HAUNTED JOPLIN

LISA LIVINGSTON-MARTIN

Published by Haunted America
A Division of The History Press
Charleston, SC 29403
www.historypress.net

Copyright © 2012 by Lisa Livingston-Martin
All rights reserved

Cover image: Photograph of the Simon Schwartz Home. Built in 1890, this home is one of many opulent buildings found in Joplin. The home was later owned by Dr. Samuel Grantham, who reportedly treated a member of Bonnie and Clyde's gang for a gunshot wound during one of their many trips through Joplin. *Photo by author.*

First published 2012

Manufactured in the United States

ISBN 978.1.60949.632.6

Library of Congress Cataloging-in-Publication Data

Livingston-Martin, Lisa.
Haunted Joplin / Lisa Livingston-Martin.
p. cm.
Includes bibliographical references.
ISBN 978-1-60949-632-6
1. Haunted places--Missouri--Joplin. 2. Ghosts--Missouri--Joplin. I. Title.
BF1472.U6L59 2012
133.109778'72--dc23
2012032999

Notice: The information in this book is true and complete to the best of our knowledge. It is offered without guarantee on the part of the author or The History Press. The author and The History Press disclaim all liability in connection with the use of this book.

All rights reserved. No part of this book may be reproduced or transmitted in any form whatsoever without prior written permission from the publisher except in the case of brief quotations embodied in critical articles and reviews.

For my children, Alex, Benton and Cameron.
May you see all your hopes and dreams come true.

CONTENTS

Acknowledgements 9

1. The Ozark Plateau: Living in a Land of Paranormal Folklore and Legend 11
2. Civil War Bullets Shape Joplin: Ghostly Soldiers 17
3. Haunted Downtown: Mobs and Lynchings 39
4. Prosperity School Bed and Breakfast: Refusing to Fade Away 53
5. The Stefflebeck Bordello: House of Horrors 63
6. Haunted Hospitals: Past and Present 67
7. The Olivia Apartments: Grand Living 73
8. Gangsters and the Serial Killer 89
9. Paranormal Mysteries and Legends 103
10. The Connor Hotel: Opulence and Tragedy 119
11. Paranormal Investigation Methods 133

Bibliography 137
About the Author 143

Acknowledgements

I have been blessed by the support of many people during this project. I would like to thank my three amazing sons, who are my inspiration and motivation, and my mother and my sisters, who have put up with the demands on my time.

My experiences with Paranormal Science Lab (PSL) have inspired this book. Follow PSL's research at www.paranormalsciencelab.com. A thank-you to all of the Paranormal Science Lab team members, whose efforts made much of this project possible: Brian Schwartz, Jordyn Cole, Mistie Cole, Eric Crinnian, Matt Crinnian, Kelly Still Harris, Bill Martin and Carla Martin.

I would also like to thank those who have been supportive of Paranormal Science Lab and its efforts to bring attention to and to promote preservation efforts for historic sites such as the Kendrick House in Carthage, Missouri.

A special thanks to Victorian Carthage, the nonprofit owner of the Kendrick House, and to its board of directors, Kelly Still Harris, Bonnie Harris and Roberta Williams, who are more than caretakers of this wonderful, historic home. Thanks also to the Joplin, Missouri Public Library, the Post Memorial Art Museum of Joplin and the Webb City Public Library. And to Danya Walker, Mike Harris, John Hacker, Joe Hadsall, Kevin McClintock, Leslie Simpson, Josh Shackles, the *Carthage Press*, *Joplin Globe*, *Joplin Metro Magazine*, *Show Me the Ozarks Magazine*, the Fuse, KOAM TV, KODE TV and the Missouri Humanities Council for spreading the word. Thanks to all of those who have attended PSL activities, including

Acknowledgements

the Haunted History Tours at the Kendrick House. We have made new friends and enjoyed sharing both history and the paranormal with the public.

I am indebted to the knowledge of many people in researching and writing this book. I want to thank Steve Cottrell, author and expert on history in southwest Missouri. I would like to thank former and current property owners and residents of locations featured in *Haunted Joplin* for speaking with me. Thanks to those who were kind enough to contribute use of their photographs: Paranormal Science Lab members; Victorian Carthage, for use of items in the Kendrick House collection; the Joplin Library; and the Post Memorial Art Museum.

I wish to extend a special thank-you to Janice Tremeear, of Springfield, Missouri, author of *Missouri's Haunted Route 66: Ghosts Along the Mother Road*, *Haunted Ozarks* and *Wicked St. Louis,* for encouragement and for introducing me to my editor, Ben Gibson. A special thank-you to Ben Gibson and everyone at The History Press, for making this book possible.

CHAPTER ONE
THE OZARK PLATEAU

LIVING IN A LAND OF PARANORMAL FOLKLORE AND LEGEND

When people discuss Joplin's origins, they usually start with the years following the Civil War, when events led many to use the name "Joplin" when referring to the growing mining settlement. As with many stories, the beginning isn't quite that simple. The area that is present-day Joplin was once settled by various Indian tribes, most notably the Osage, until the Osage War of 1836 pushed the tribe west into the Kansas and Oklahoma territories. The name "Ozarks" is derived from the Osage Indians.

White settlers came into the area beginning in the 1830s. Various settlements and towns were formed in the area of the future city of Joplin. John Cox, who, along with Patrick Murphy, would come to found the city of Joplin, first founded the city of Blytheville in 1836, in what is now north central Joplin. Like most settlers coming into southwest Missouri during the 1830s, Cox was a southerner. He built a log cabin for his family, and a small settlement grew up around his property. After the establishment of a post office in 1841, the settlement was named Blytheville. Soon, other settlers were establishing large tracts of property, and other settlements formed, one of which was Sherwood, which stood on the northwest edge of present-day Joplin. At the outbreak of the Civil War, Sherwood was the third largest town in Jasper County, with more than 250 residents.

Over time, Native American legends from the region and the beliefs of southern settlers converged to give the Ozark Plateau region a rich, unique folklore, including documentation of paranormal experiences. As a result,

The Sigar family, early settlers of Joplin. Notice that Joplin is written on the oxen yoke. *Courtesy of the Joplin Public Library.*

events of long ago continue to reverberate in the form of paranormal activity in certain places, and today, the observer is left with the task of deciphering the activity's origins and meaning.

There are some recurrent ghost stories told throughout the Ozark Plateau area that date to the 1800s. There are numerous stories of old, haunted log cabins that involve noises heard by passersby—sounds of someone chopping wood, of an axe being sharpened on a grindstone and even that of water being poured on the grindstone in intervals, as would have been done in life. These stories were recounted in various places and usually involved abandoned cabins and farmhouses. Other types of noises discussed in these early ghost tales include that of a man walking across the floor in his boots and retrieving water from a bucket. This story has been associated with abandoned homes as well as occupied dwellings. For instance, in the 1900s, an elderly woman claimed to have heard the sound of a man's boots crossing her floor and of water being dipped from a bucket in her small log cabin.

In other instances, the cabin itself was the ghost. People have claimed to have seen phantom cabins in the distance in spots where no building ever existed, as far as local residents could recall. These visions would appear and vanish as one approached them, almost like a mirage. Another common story would involve travelers observing smoke coming from the chimney of an unoccupied cabin, and upon inspection, they would find that the floor was covered in thick, undisturbed dust and that no fire had been built in the fireplace in years. Likewise, the phantom cabins described were often said to have smoke rising from the chimneys.

Paschal B. Randolph recounts an encounter with the paranormal in Joplin in the first decade of the twentieth century:

> GHOSTS THAT CAME WITH THE PURITANS: LITHOBOLIAC POLTERGEISTS. *They are well defined as invisible entities that throw stones, bricks, etc. at residences, as well as the people within…The author knows of this matter from personal experience and in company of several others. In the first decade of this century, I was working in the mines near Joplin, Missouri, to pay my tuition through medical college. There were several ancient log houses [near] by that were allegedly haunted. Neighbors gave them a wide berth after dark. In some of them, built in the old Baldknobber days, many bloody crimes had been committed, so said the local old timers. At that time, I was in my early twenties and boasted I was not afraid of God, man or the devil. The senseless arrogance of youth! One night in a certain log house changed all that. That is just a portion of one night. As I think back over the years, it seems to me that no more fearless set of men lived than the zinc and lead miners of the Joplin mining district. Always ready for a fight or a frolic. One [a]utumn night when the moon was full and so brilliant one could see*

While fortunes were made from the mining district around Joplin, many still lived in poverty and deplorable conditions. *Reenactment photo. Courtesy of Paranormal Science Lab.*

his shadow, five of us young fools boasted that we had no fear about one particular log cabin known as an old hang out for Baldknobbers back in Reconstruction Days that followed the Civil War. As I have said, the moon was as brilliant as man ever saw. The log cabin was on a clearing of at least 100 acres. The ground was a mixture of clay and what was called "hawg-chawed flint." This type of flint never breaks straight, but only a jagged surface is ever seen. The nearest place where one could find a rounded boulder was in Spring River, two miles away. We went in and seated ourselves on the rotting floor, at about 10 o'clock p.m [sic]. We joked and laughed nervously for about half an hour. The laughter stopped suddenly when a barrage of rocks bombarded the cabin, inside and out. We looked through the door and window openings—nobody was in sight, although a man a quarter mile away would have been perfectly visible. Then stones and dirt began to strike all of us but without much physical pain. Whether it was our excited minds or not, we seemed to hear weird noises like moans, and the sound of blows given on invisible bodies. Pandemonium! Panic! With one accord, we rushed for the single door like Old Nick himself was at our heels. Whoever, or whatever it was, we got back safely to the boarding house, short of breath and with blanched faces. In daylight, we returned to find that the stones that had assaulted us, were rounded, glacial boulders from Spring River two miles distant.

This is a detailed, firsthand account, unlike most ghost stories, and it also has context that creates a reasonable basis for activity in that location.

The Baldknobbers were a post–Civil War band of Confederate sympathizers who continued guerrilla warfare tactics to harass, frighten and often torture newly freed slaves. They operated farther east in the vicinity of Branson, Hollister and Ozark, Missouri, and gained a widespread reputation for their brutality, so the name Baldknobber quickly became a generic term for such activity. However, there were other bands of vigilantes also conducting bushwhacker-style atrocities, so these "bloody crimes" may have been organized by a group like the Baldknobbers or by a gang of local criminals. This area had seen service by the Kansas Second Infantry, the first black Union unit to see combat in the Civil War. The infantry was based in Baxter Springs, Kansas, and many of its black soldiers were escaped slaves from western Jasper County, Missouri (now Joplin). There had been tragic results, including the Rader Farm Massacre and the burning of the town of Sherwood due to mistreatment of the bodies of slain black soldiers in the area. Both of these events resulted in deep bitterness that carried over into the Reconstruction era.

While tales of Baldknobber violence may have been invented by the old-timers to scare young men, the fact that neighbors avoided the area at night suggests that something had indeed transpired at the cabin. If Mr. Randolph is correct and he and his companions were able to clearly view the land surrounding the cabin for one-fourth of a mile, it seems unlikely that someone followed them to the cabin and threw dirt and stones at them. It also seems unlikely that someone would have carried rocks from two miles away for the prank, especially someone on foot. Additionally, it is more likely that the reported noise of someone receiving a beating was paranormal activity rather than an act by pranksters. If someone staged the events for Randolph and his friends to hear, that person (or persons) would have been close by and would have presumably been observed through the door and windows. This event also occurred at a time prior to anyone having an available means of prerecording sounds to be replayed later. A phonograph recording would still have to have been played by someone winding the crank by hand if the event were a prank, and the phonograph itself would most likely have been seen. The fact that the stones were present the next day indicates that the men did have an experience outside of the normal.

Another recurring haunting in the Ozarks involves animals, most often a large black dog. This phantom dog follows people silently and exhibits the normal movements of a dog. Some versions of the story describe the dog as headless. The significance of the dog being headless is uncertain, although early accounts usually state that the witnesses are frightened and unsettled by that fact. It appears that in certain versions, the apparition of the black dog is understood to be an omen of death.

On a personal note, such a black dog phantom was observed by a family member of mine shortly before my father passed away. Ironically, my father's favorite dog had been a large, all-black German shepherd named Rommel who weighed over 150 pounds. When he sat down, he resembled a bear. Although he looked menacing to strangers, he was extremely gentle and loyal to my father. Rommel died about fifteen years prior to the following events. A family member was mowing a pasture on the family farm when he noticed a black dog following the tractor at a distance. At first, he assumed a neighbor's dog had wandered into the pasture, but the dog continued to follow the tractor, round after round, through the pasture. Rommel had followed my father everywhere as he worked on the farm, including following the tractor for hours at a time if my dad was driving, although he wouldn't if someone else was on the tractor. As this family member started paying more attention to the dog, he recognized his lope and the way his tongue hung out of the side of his mouth. He relayed his experience to me that day and was visibly unsettled by what he observed. He was convinced that he had watched Rommel follow my dad's tractor for at least a couple of hours. My father was very ill at the time and passed away a few months later. The family member believed that Rommel was waiting for my dad.

A similar story of an animal phantom arose during the Civil War. Soldiers would tell stories about seeing a huge phantom wild boar. This apparition became associated with the death of the observer, which usually occurred within a week's time. One account tells of a soldier who saw the ghost boar the night before an intense battle. The night after the battle, he boasted that he had beaten the curse since he survived the battle. However, he was killed that night by the accidental discharge of a comrade's gun.

Traditionally, there was a strong belief in witchcraft in the Ozarks region, which fostered a fear of ghosts and the belief that haunted places were evil. It was common for early settlers to take precautions against witches that may cross their paths. One such precaution was the use of a witch peg, a charm found in rural areas of the Ozarks that was used to keep witches from entering a home. Often a witch peg was made from cedar wood, which was generally used by traditional societies in Europe and by Native Americans as a means of protection against evil spirits and negative influences. The peg had three prongs and was driven into the ground in the path to the door. According to folklore, the prongs represented the Christian Trinity. It was considered bad luck to step on or disturb a witch peg.

Vance Randolph, who was an expert on Ozark folklore, chronicled these beliefs in *Ozark Magic and Folklore* (1964). At the time Randolph's book was published, witchcraft was still perceived to be a real threat: the danger was thought to be ever-present and could come in the form of seemingly innocent activities, such as teaching schoolchildren to recite their multiplication tables (forward or backward) from memory. This particular example was viewed by many as antichristian, as it was thought that witches recited the Lord's Prayer backward during their ceremonies. According to Randolph, one "pious Baptist lady" in McDonald County, Missouri, disapproved of the local schoolteacher for teaching the girls in her care their multiplication tables in such a way because of the danger that "they'll be a-sayin' somethin' else back-lards [sic] tomorrow." This general sentiment led many to avoid places known to be haunted and to speak of such things in hushed tones.

CHAPTER TWO
CIVIL WAR BULLETS SHAPE JOPLIN

GHOSTLY SOLDIERS

To say that Joplin started as a unified city founded in 1873 would be to overlook some of the most violent events in its history—events that still linger in some of the city's haunted places. The fact that there were Civil War battles on the ground where Joplin stands today comes as a surprise to many of Joplin's own residents. The tough and strong personalities that dominated the Joplin mining district in later years were often forged in the fire of war.

ROTHANBARGER HOUSE:
GHOSTLY TALES OF ANTEBELLUM MISSOURI

Solomon Rothanbarger, an immigrant from Pennsylvania, arrived at Turkey Creek (located in present-day Joplin, Missouri) in 1839 and staked out a homestead at the age of nineteen on the creek's banks, which would one day be in the eastern part of Joplin. In 1850, he left his wife to tend to their farm and went to California to seek his fortune in the gold rush. He was met with success and returned a year later with enough money to finance a burgeoning construction and brickworks business, which became Rothanbarger & Sons, and to build a brick mansion. The brickworks were located on-site at his Turkey Creek property. Construction on the Rothanbarger House started in about 1851, and today, it is one of the oldest standing homes in the Joplin

Southwest Missouri, known to both armies as the "burnt district," was reshaped economically and demographically by the Civil War, with more battles and skirmishes occurring in Missouri than any other state, except for Virginia and Tennessee. Many towns disappeared under the scorched-earth policies used by both sides. *Reenactment photo. Courtesy of Paranormal Science Lab.*

area. The home faces southward, overlooking the low river valley. The house is smaller than it is perceived from the street that runs alongside the property. The house is also known as the "History House."

The mansion was built in the Federal style, which was popular at the time. It features four rooms, two on the first floor and two above. There is an original brick addition on the rear of the house, the east side, which served as the kitchen. On closer inspection of the handmade brick, one can see gray bricks that appear to have been glazed interspersed among the red bricks in a deliberate pattern. The glazing occurred when a brick was placed too close to a hot spot in the wood-fired kilns and the silica in the river clay was liquefied.

It has long been believed that the home was finished in the early 1850s. However, recently discovered Rothanbarger family correspondence indicates that the house was originally a one-story home and that the second story was added later, perhaps after the Civil War. It is not evident from the front or sidewalls of the house that the second story was a later addition. However, looking at the rear wall from a distance, there appears to be a line in the brick, at which the colors are slightly different; the differences are uniform enough to suggest that two different types of clay were used in making the bricks for this wall. The reason for different clays is not known, as river clay in this area is fairly uniform in appearance and readily available on-site. While it is not certain at this point when the house was finished to match its present-day appearance, it is clear that the home was the site of Civil War events. It was used as a field hospital on multiple occasions during fighting and skirmishes in the vicinity, reputedly by both the Federals and Confederates, housing up to thirteen wounded soldiers at once. It is unclear whether soldiers died in the home, although it is a realistic possibility.

Mrs. Rothanbarger died in the middle of a harsh winter, and the ground was frozen solid, so a grave could not be dug. (This was before the use of morticians and embalming, and graves had to be dug by hand.) The family had no choice but to postpone a funeral until the ground thawed. Mrs. Rothanbarger was put in the west bedroom upstairs. The windows were opened to allow the cold air in the room. It was in this manner that Mrs. Rothanbarger waited two months to be buried, and perhaps, she still lingers there.

Rothanbarger House is the oldest standing house in Joplin and one of only a handful of pre–Civil War homes that survived the burnings during the war. Scorch marks can be seen over the porch where bushwhackers set the porch on fire trying to burn the house down during the Civil War. *Courtesy of the author.*

For 160 years, the Rothanbarger House remained a private residence, which is very unusual for a home in southwest Missouri, as so few survived the Civil War. Paranormal activity has been observed for years. The current owners have observed an apparition of a woman in nineteenth-century clothing walking through the kitchen, and the kitchen has been in the same location since the house was built. An apparition of a man has been observed in the addition from the yard through the windows that, on first glance, appeared to be a live person, startling the owner. Knocking on the back door and wall has been so loud and pronounced that it could be heard at the other end of a phone conversation. Footsteps have been heard in the hallway upstairs, and people have been startled awake in the east bedroom with the sensation that they were being poked in the side by an unseen hand.

In his book *Haunted Ozark Battlefields*, Steve Cottrell relates an event that he witnessed at the Rothanbarger House in the 1980s, when the house was owned by another couple. After a living-history event, in which Cottrell was a reenactor, some of the participants decided to conduct a séance in the dining room. Cottrell elected to retire to the parlor and eventually dozed off to sleep on the couch. He was awakened by the sound of breaking glass in the same room, followed by the emotional sobbing and muttering of several participants of the séance in the dining room. Upon investigation, he discovered a round piece of glass had popped out of the side of an oil lamp that was sitting on the mantel. Cottrell also related that his friends said they did see a ghost once in the house: a vaporous mist moving down a hallway.

The current owners informed me that they have been visited by Rothanbarger family descendants, who related that Solomon Rothanbarger's property was utilized as a stop on the Underground Railroad. This is plausible since Rothanbarger was known to be a Union man. According to the Rothanbarger descendants, there was a cave that was almost directly south of the home that overlooked Turkey Creek, and it was used to hide runaway slaves on their journey to freedom. It is likely that they would have been en route to Kansas, less than fifteen miles to the west, as many northern sympathizers in southwest Missouri migrated to Kansas to escape the violence and harsh living conditions, which grew worse as the war continued. Many of the black soldiers in the Kansas First Volunteers who were stationed at Baxter Springs were escaped slaves from southwest Missouri.

There is also a story of Confederate bushwhackers setting fire to the front porch in an attempt to burn the house down—a common practice in the guerrilla-style warfare that was employed in southwest Missouri.

Women were often left to provide for their children and hold the family together while the men were off fighting. *Reenactment photo. Courtesy of Paranormal Science Lab.*

Scorch marks are still visible on the bricks around and above the porch, extending well above the level of the floor of the second story. It does not appear that the front wall of the home has been altered or extended upward, and it would seem to indicate that if the newly discovered Rothanbarger family correspondence is correct—that the second story was added sometime after the war—the scorch marks are from a later fire. There is no clear evidence that the story of bushwhackers setting fire to the porch is mistaken either. The owner showed me where Civil War–era musket balls had been embedded into the west outer wall of the home, including one that was still firmly embedded in the brick, but whether the musket balls are from a porch-burning incident is unknown. It is also said that Jesse and Frank James hid out in the Spring House by the creek in the valley below the house. The James brothers are known to have been in the area at various times while riding with the guerrilla William Quantrill.

The Rothanbarger House served as a field hospital on multiple occasions, especially for Union soldiers. During one such stint as a hospital, there were nine Union soldiers convalescing from injuries when Southern

Bushwhackers and outlaws made an impression in many places in the area, not only during the Civil War but also in the years that followed. *Reenactment photo. Courtesy of Paranormal Science Lab.*

bushwhackers were spotted on their way to the Rothanbarger home. The men hurriedly dressed, saddled their horses and left for Greenfield, where there was a Union garrison. In their haste, one man rode the entire forty-plus miles without his trousers. It wasn't a foolish move either, as the bushwhackers pursued them for a number of miles. Another story that centers on the Rothanbarger House involved another wounded Union soldier, but this man was too ill to ride or attempt a getaway. Instead, the Confederates loaded him up on a wagon, and official accounts state that the wagon was stopped not too far south so that the Union soldier could be hanged from a tree near the road. It is believed the Confederates were on their way to Neosho, which remained a Confederate garrison and refugee camp throughout most of the war. While the location of this hanging is not officially known, it may have been in the Royal Heights area of Joplin, to the west of the Rothanbarger House. The stagecoach road went through the middle of present-day Royal Heights, and there was a stop for the stagecoach there.

Royal Heights Haunting: Poltergeist with a Civil War Connection?

During an investigation of a private home in the Royal Heights area, Paranormal Science Lab (PSL) discovered a Civil War connection to activity in the home, a connection that was not known before the investigation. PSL was called to the home due to paranormal activity that centered on a two-year-old child. For descriptive purposes, the boy will be referred to as "Bobby."

The boy's parents had lived in the house for several years before their son was born, and over time, unusual things began to occur. Unexplained noises were the predominant activity. After Bobby's birth, activity became more intense and more frequent. From the time Bobby could talk, he referred to someone by name, someone or something he called "Jackson," and he appeared to interact with someone. Bobby's parents assumed that this was an imaginary friend and were not immediately concerned. Over time, Bobby became vigilant while taking baths and would watch the corners of the room by the ceiling, following something around the top of the room with his eyes and speaking to Jackson. It wasn't very long before Bobby became wary of Jackson and indicated that Jackson was mean. Eventually, he would refuse to take a bath in the house. The most aggressive paranormal activity occurred when his mother found Bobby sitting in the middle of the floor with the mattress flipped out of his bed. Bobby's mother had heard the thud and ran into the room to check on him. The mattress, however, sat inside the frame of the bed and would have had to have been lifted at least a foot over the boy's head for the mattress to come out of the frame. The mattress was also fairly heavy, and it seems doubtful that Bobby could have managed this feat on his own. If this was a paranormal event, it appears to have been caused by a poltergeist, which is German for "noisy ghost." Poltergeist activity is characterized by the moving or throwing of objects.

In an interview, Bobby's parents told PSL that the tree in the front yard is thought to be a hanging tree used during the Civil War. Their next-door neighbor's family originally owned the lots where the couple's house now sits. The neighbor's ninety-five-year-old mother grew up next door. She told the PSL team that when she was a young girl, she was told that the tree was used as a hanging tree during the Civil War, but she did not know any more than that. The tree is about four feet in diameter, making it possible that it is over 150 years old. However, the fact that the tree is still standing bothered me. The area immediately surrounding the house was inhabited before the Civil War, and there was an active stagecoach line within yards of the tree. The fact that the tree was near the old stagecoach road made the story of the wounded soldier's hanging at this spot plausible. However, it was customary in the region to cut down a tree that had been used for hanging because it was considered to be unlucky or cursed. Jasper County suffered a drastic decline in population during the Civil War, going from over six thousand residents prior to the war to an estimated thirty or forty persons at its end. It is possible that no one was available to cut the tree down.

It was also discovered that the house was built in the 1930s but sustained heavy fire damage in the late 1940s. Records indicate that there were no fatalities in the fire. The house was renovated and an addition was added in the 1940s. The house has been occupied ever since. No confirmed deaths in the house were discovered. PSL focused its investigation on Bobby's bedroom and the adjoining bathroom.

Paranormal Science Lab members Lisa Livingston-Martin (left) and Kelly Harris (right) in period clothing. PSL conducts history tours and paranormal investigations for the public in historic sites. Photo taken at Kendrick House, Carthage, Missouri. *Courtesy of Paranormal Science Lab.*

An electronic voice phenomena (EVP) session was conducted. An EVP is a voice or other sound recorded on audio devices, which was not heard at the time of the recording. When the question "Do you like the little boy that sleeps in here?" was asked, an EVP of a man's voice replied, "No."

The next question was "Do you like Bobby?" An EVP captured a stern reply: "Yeah."

Shortly afterward, during a pause in the EVP session, a second man's voice said, "Out."

One of the investigators asked, "Is someone being mean to Bobby?"

"No," the second man's voice replied.

Later, an investigator was walking through the house carrying a video camera. As he walked through the bathroom, another voice was captured by the video camera, saying urgently, "Doctor!" However, the investigator did not hear a voice as he walked through the bathroom. Whether this was the sick Union soldier taken from the Rothanbarger House seeking medical attention only to be hanged instead is unknown. However, it is possible, considering the soldiers would likely have passed by as there were few roads in the area.

The Rader Farm Massacre and the Burning of Sherwood

As the Civil War approached, lead mining was already an important part of the local economy. Most of the men living in the area ended up fighting in one of the two armies or serving as guerrilla fighters in a partisan ranger unit. Thomas Livingston owned the mine at Minersville (now Oronogo) in western Jasper County, which in time became the largest lead and zinc mine in the world; today, it is known as Oronogo Circle. When the war broke out, it is said that Livingston dumped several thousand pounds of molten lead into Center Creek at his smelter in Minersville to prevent approaching Federal troops from confiscating it for making ammunition. He and his half brother, William Parkinson, also had a lead smelter at French Point, which was several miles west of Minersville and also on Center Creek. They also had a store and mill.

Livingston also held stakes in the lead mines at Granby in Newton County, which was the largest lead-producing mining district in southwest Missouri at the outbreak of the war. The Confederate army occupied

Guerrilla fighters played a significant role during the Civil War, either terrorizing civilians or protecting them. *Reenactment photo. Courtesy of Paranormal Science Lab.*

Granby until they were forced out of southwest Missouri after the Battle of Pea Ridge in 1862. The strategic value of the Granby mines was such that official Confederate reports tracked the tonnage of lead being shipped to Fort Smith, Arkansas, and boasted that the commanding officer in Granby was confident that the Granby mines would supply the Confederacy's demand for lead for bullets. Two hundred thousand pounds of lead per month were shipped from Granby. The Civil War changed Thomas Livingston from a businessman to a guerrilla fighter, and he was called a bushwhacker by his enemies.

George B. Walker, a local resident, wrote of Thomas Livingston after the war, saying that he "never knew fear and his men during the war idolized him. They said that there was never a leader so good to his men as Major Tom Livingston." Livingston and his men enlisted in the provisional army of the Confederate States and were designated as the First Battalion Missouri Cavalry (also known as the First Indian Brigade), and the group would come to be known as the Cherokee Spikes (sometimes called the Bloody Spikes).

By late July 1861, Livingston and his men were patrolling the Missouri-Kansas border and were also protecting the lead mines at Granby and Minersville. As the war wore on and the Confederacy failed to devote resources to the border area, Livingston sent requests to the Confederate command, requesting additional resources and men to protect the people from further peril. Livingston engaged in negotiations with Union commanders who were operating in the region, attempting to secure mutual assurances to not disrupt farmers and to allow the planting of crops without the risk of fields being torched. These actions indicate that Livingston had motives beyond mere plunder, revenge or military objectives. They also drew the condemnation of some of his Confederate superiors.

The event that stands out the most with Thomas R. Livingston's operations is the Rader Farm Massacre in western Jasper County, Missouri, and the consequences of the events there. Fort Blair, a wooden fort, had been built in Baxter Springs, Kansas, by the Union army as a means of protecting the supply trains traveling the military road between Fort Scott in Kansas, which was some fifty miles north, and Fort Gibson in Indian Territory approximately one hundred miles to the south. Fort Blair sat a mere fifteen miles inside Kansas and was due west of present-day Joplin, Missouri.

The guerrilla warfare that raged in southwest Missouri did not stop after the war. Many guerrilla fighters like Frank and Jesse James simply employed what they learned fighting in the Civil War to pursue a profit through bank robberies and other criminal activities. *Reenactment photo. Courtesy of Paranormal Science Lab.*

The Union raised an all-black regiment at Baxter Springs called the First Kansas Colored Infantry. Many of the soldiers were escaped slaves from southwest Missouri. These black troops were under the command of James Williams. The First Kansas was the second colored unit that was officially mustered into service for the Union but was the first colored unit to see combat and suffer casualties in the Civil War at the Battle of Mound Island in October 1862. The battle took place near Butler in Bates County, Missouri, along the northern edge of the "burnt district," as southwest Missouri came to be called as a result of the scorched-earth policies employed by both the Union and the Confederacy in that area.

Williams was anxious to prove the ability of his men, and perhaps this contributed to a rash decision to send them into Jasper County on May 6, 1863, to forage for food. The column was hard to miss, having wagons, infantry and cavalry, all of which seems ill suited for foraging for food behind enemy lines. The troops raided homes, taking a carding machine, which was used to turn cotton into thread, and Mrs. Scott, the lady of the house, was held for a time. A wagon of flour that was on its way to Livingston's men was taken from a young boy who was driving the wagon, and he was also held and later released along with Mrs. Scott. After capturing twenty horses and mules, two local women rode into the Federal line. When Major Ward asked what they were doing, the women answered that they were counting his men to tell Livingston how many soldiers were encamped. Ward confiscated the ladies' horses, and while walking out of the Federal camp, the ladies said they were still delivering the information to Livingston. The next morning, the women returned and demanded the return of their horses and saddles. Ward again refused, and they complained loudly and in particular to Hugh Thompson, one of the Union soldiers whom they knew, threatening that Livingston and his men would hang him when they returned. Next, Williams's men camped at the home of R.R. Twitty, one of Livingston's men, and took three hundred pounds of bacon, a calf and corn from Twitty's mother.

Williams didn't merely send the men into Missouri: he sent them to Sherwood, which, aside from being the third largest town in Jasper County, was known as a strong Confederate enclave. Many of the men fighting under Livingston lived at Sherwood. But Williams didn't stop there. On May 11, 1863, he sent an insulting letter to Livingston, in which he failed to even address Livingston by name:

To Commanding officer of Southern forces in Jasper & Newton County, MO,

Sir,
I came here by order of my Superiors under instructions to put a stop to the Guerilla [sic] *or Bushwacking* [sic] *war which is now being carried out by the enemies of the United States in Jasper and Newton Counties, MO. It is my desire in this Business to follow as far as practicable all the rules applicable to Civilized warfare. I there propose that you collect all the enemies of the United States in your vicinity and come to some point and attack me, or give me notice where I can find your force and I will fight you on your own ground.*

But if you persist in the System of Guerilla warfare heretofore followed by you and refuse to fight openly like soldiers fighting for a cause I feel bound to treat you as thieves and robbers who lurk in secret places fighting only defenseless people and wholly unworthy the fate due to Chivalrous Soldiers engaged in honorable warfare. And I shall take any means within my power to rid the Country of your murderous Gang.

Earnestly yours,
J.M. Williams
Col 1st KS Col Vols

Williams's choice of words was ironic in light of the plundering and theft his men had committed in Jasper County in the week prior to this letter. The week following this letter saw Livingston and Union Major Eno's men clashing in Jasper County along Center Creek just west of Minersville. Williams was challenging Livingston to a fight, but Livingston just vanished after the six-day running fight with Union Major Eno. On May 18, 1863, having received no reply to his letter, Williams ordered a portion of the First Kansas Colored back into Jasper County on a second foraging detail around Sherwood. Again, this was impetuous on Williams's part, as many of the men in the foraging party were unarmed, and they made up a much smaller detail than the one from the previous week. The same day, Livingston's scouts reported there were sixty soldiers from the First Kansas foraging near Sherwood, Missouri. Livingston led sixty-seven of his "best mounted men" to engage the Federal troops.

The Rader Farm was also a significant target from a psychological perspective, as the ten-room wood-framed farmhouse was the largest and most impressive home in western Jasper County and one of the best examples of a prosperous Confederate citizen. In other words, Williams and Ward were making a statement by raiding this particular farm and taking its

Soldiers often lived off the land and what they could confiscate, which imposed additional hardships on the local residents. *Reenactment photo. Courtesy of Paranormal Science Lab.*

food stores and supplies. We can only speculate as to why Williams sent a far smaller force than he had on the first foraging mission twelve days earlier: a mere twenty-five men of the First Kansas and twenty men of the Second Kansas Battery.

Major Ward found a large supply of corn hidden in the upstairs rooms of the farmhouse. Although Ward took the precaution of setting pickets, he took the extra step of driving Mrs. Rader and her daughters off of her property, instead of the normal practice of confiscating supplies while the women stood watching. It's possible he anticipated that the women would send word to Livingston and draw the Confederate guerrillas into a confrontation. A wagon was brought to the south side of the house, and a lieutenant called for twenty of the black soldiers to leave their muskets along the fence and to throw the corn and valuables in the house out of the second-story windows and into the wagon.

Livingston's men had cut off the six men on picket duty and were able to surprise the Federal troops at the Rader farmhouse. Three Union soldiers were killed within minutes, and another three white soldiers as well as two black soldiers were captured. When the shooting started, two white soldiers and the rest of the black soldiers were still in the house. Running outside, the white men escaped, but the black men were shot down "before [even] taking a dozen steps."

After the battle, Mrs. Vivion saw one Union wagon with two men racing back toward her house and called out, asking about the rest of the Union soldiers. One man yelled back, "Shot to hell!" Mrs. Rader packed a wagon and took her daughters south to Texas that evening. Her husband was later killed in battle. The Rader family never returned to Missouri.

Livingston sent a report to General Sterling Price on the whole affair:

> *On the 18th, my scouts reported 60 negroes and white men, belonging to Colonel Williams['s] negro regiment, with five six-mule teams [wagons], foraging on Centre Creek Prairie. I ordered out 67 of my best-mounted men. I came upon them at Mrs. Rad[e]r's, pillaging her premises. I afterward learned that they were ordered not to take more plunder than they could take with them. I charged them at the house, flanking them on the right, routed them, and pursued them about 8 miles, to the crossing of Spring River. The enemy's loss in killed was, negroes 23, and 7 white men, wounded, unknown; and prisoners: also captured 30 mules and five wagons; a box containing 1,400 cartridges and caps, a good many guns, pistols &...I sustained no loss.*

Williams learned of the battle at Rader Farm late in the day and ordered out five companies and some cavalry—almost four hundred men. They marched from Baxter Springs through the night, reaching Sherwood at daylight. When the Union men reached the Rader Farm, they found the bodies of the black soldiers where they had fallen the day before. They gathered the bodies that they could find (eleven in all), placed them in the house and prepared to set it on fire.

Delaying the order, Williams made another inflammatory move at this point. Williams and his men came upon John Bishop, who was coming from Fort Scott. Bishop, forty-seven years old, was one of Livingston's men who had been taken prisoner in the autumn of 1862. He had been released a couple of days before from Fort Lincoln, twelve miles north of Fort Scott and approximately seventy miles from the Sherwood area, and was walking home in a pair of U.S. government–issued shoes. Unfortunately for Bishop, some of Williams's men recognized him and told Williams that Bishop was found near the scene of the massacre with a weapon. Williams had Bishop marched into the Rader farmhouse and shot, and his body was thrown on top of those of the black soldiers. Williams later wrote of Bishop, "I felt it to be my duty to shoot him on the spot and he was accordingly summarily executed."

Williams then had the Rader farmhouse torched in full view of the residents of Sherwood and ordered that "everything in a five-mile radius be burned." At least twelve farms were burned, and the entire town of Sherwood (a population of 250 and the only leading commercial center left in Jasper County) was burned to the ground, never to be rebuilt. Where there were families living in houses, the occupants were given a few minutes to grab what possessions they could carry before the house was set on fire. Mrs. Vivion and her daughter Eliza were among those who hurriedly packed some possessions into a wagon and headed south to Texas, just as Mrs. Rader had the night before.

Williams's decision to burn the bodies of his soldiers is shrouded in controversy. It was not the policy of the Union to burn its dead soldiers; instead, when a large number of soldiers were killed and their bodies could

Residents had no choice but to stand by and watch as Union soldiers torched farms and the entire town of Sherwood. Many left the area and never returned. *Reenactment photo. Courtesy of Paranormal Science Lab.*

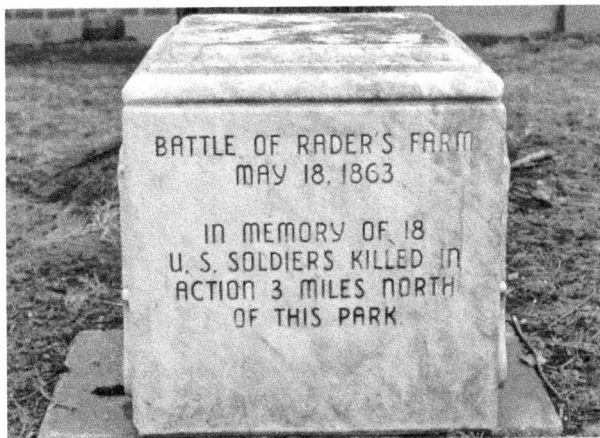

This monument was erected to commemorate soldiers who were killed at the Rader Farm Massacre. It sits in front of the museum complex in Schifferdecker Park. *Courtesy of the author.*

not be returned to a post, they were placed in mass graves. Williams and some of his men later claimed they felt it was necessary because they didn't have time to dig graves or return the bodies to Fort Blair due to the danger of another attack by Livingston. This explanation seems hollow considering that Williams took time to burn farms and an entire town, even allowing residents to first remove their belongings from their homes. Moreover, the bodies of the white soldiers who died at the Rader Farm were not burned. The Rader Farm Massacre was the worst loss to a black unit up to that point in the war.

If Williams had planned on provoking a response with his foraging parties, it was his men who suffered the consequences. The black soldiers who died at Rader Farm suffered a level of brutality not often seen, even in such a brutal war. No doubt, the scene Williams found contributed to his imprudent decision to burn the bodies of his men. Williams described the scene:

> *I visited the scene of the engagement the morning after its occurrence. And for the first time beheld the horrible evidences of the demoniac [sic] spirit of these rebel fiends in their treatment of our dead and wounded. Men were found with their brains beaten out with clubs, and the bloody weapons left at their sides, and their bodies most horribly mutilated.*

Williams's writings after the war indicate that some of the participants on the Confederate side at Rader Farm were actually residents of the area or men who were not part of Livingston's unit. It is unknown whether these brutal acts of desecration were deeds committed by Livingston's men or by local residents.

The burning of Rader Farm and of Sherwood would ultimately play out in national politics and also in strategy in western Jasper County, Missouri. The Union had only started using black troops in combat the previous fall, and the official Confederate response was to proclaim that black soldiers would not be viewed as enemy soldiers or prisoners of war but rather as escaped slaves, implying that they could be killed or pressed into slavery. In response, President Lincoln ordered that if Union soldiers who were taken as prisoners were not treated as prisoners of war, then the Union would respond similarly in its treatment of Confederate soldiers; in essence, Lincoln was advocating an "eye-for-an-eye" policy, which he felt necessary in order to deter the atrocious treatment of black soldiers. Williams received his response the following day in the form of the following letter from Thomas Livingston:

> *Camp Jackson May 20th 1863*
> *Col Williams, honored sir*
> *I have five of your Sol[di]ers prisoners three Whi[te] and two Black men. The whi[te] men I propose Exchanging with you if you have any of My men or other confederate Sol[di]ers to exchange for Them. [A]s for the Negros I cannot recognize them as Sol[di]ers and, in cons[e]quence I will hav[e] to hold them as contrabands of war. [I]f my proposals S[ui]tes your will, return immediately my men or other Confederate sol[di]ers and I will send you your men. You arrested a citizen of this neighborhood by the name of Bishop. If that is your mode of warfare to arrest civil citizens who are living at home and trying to raise a crop for their families, let me know and I will try to play to your hand. Mr. Bishop was once arrested, taken to Fort Scott examined, released and passed home a civil citizen. Some of your men stated that he was burnt up in Mrs. Rader's house, but I am satisfied that you are too high-toned a gentleman to stoop, or condescend to such brutal deeds of barbarity.*
> *I remain yours truly,*
> *T.R. Livingston Maj comdg confederate forces*
> [First Missouri Cavalry Battalion]

A black soldier being held prisoner by Livingston was killed in camp. Livingston contended that a man who did not belong to his unit came into the camp and killed the Union soldier. Williams held Livingston responsible and later wrote that he and Livingston met face to face to negotiate the issue, but he claimed that he was not satisfied by Livingston's version of the events. Williams made good on his promise to execute a prisoner in response to the death of the black soldier in Livingston's camp. One of Livingston's men who was being held as a prisoner at Fort Lincoln was marched outside of the fort and summarily shot. These events marked the first occasion that the policy to respond in kind when black soldiers were not afforded the conventions of prisoner-of-war status was carried out.

Livingston and his men attacked the Missouri Militia at Stockton, Missouri, on July 11, 1863. During the engagement, Livingston was shot next to the courthouse while leading the assault. He fell from his horse, and as Livingston tried to rise, several Union soldiers emerged from the courthouse. One of the Union solders picked up Livingston's pistol and struck him with a horrific blow to the head. Several others fired into his body. Livingston's body and those of two of his men were left on the courthouse lawn as Livingston's men retreated. Livingston is said to be buried in an unmarked grave in the cemetery at Stockton, Missouri.

A couple of days later, one of Livingston's men, Tom Webb, returned to Stockton and was able to retrieve two of the three dead men. There is speculation that one of those bodies was that of Thomas Livingston. Various sources indicate that Webb returned to Jasper County and buried the men on his property, which was situated just north of that of Solomon Rothanbarger. A week later, Union troops rode onto Webb's farm, walked him and his teenage son Austin into the woods and shot them in the back of the heads. Webb's wife and younger son found the bodies, and the boy went to Rothanbarger, who returned with a wagon and helped the boy bury his father and brother. Later, the two Webbs were reinterred in the Webb City Cemetery.

The Webb City Cemetery is known to have "graveyard lights" or "ghost lights," which are said to occur throughout the Ozarks. They are often seen in cemeteries and appear as balls of light dancing around the tombstones. These are said to be the spirits of those interred in the cemetery, particularly those who died tragically or who died so fast that their souls don't know they had passed on.

People shied away from the site of the burnt Rader farmhouse and the memories of the burnt men. Stories of the site being haunted by the ghosts of the men who died there spread in the years that followed. About twenty years after the war, a family moved onto the land, ignoring the legends that the area was haunted, and built a house on the foundation of the Rader house. They lived there and farmed successfully until some fifty years later, when the house mysteriously burned. The family decided not to rebuild, and the site of the Rader house was never built on again.

If you stand at the side of the road and look across the now open pasture that is dotted by two ponds, you can see the slight depression in the earth where the foundation of the farmhouse rested. The sight inspires a heavy feeling, the kind you experience in hallowed places known as sites of sacrifice. But there are no signs or monuments here—just empty space. Other buildings have been built nearby, including a now old, dilapidated school building that is owned by the county and that is also said to be a place of odd happenings (though these are generally attributed to trespassers and kids). The locked door stands open repeatedly, and the entrance shows signs of scorching and smoke damage. It may well be vandalism, but as many current residents don't know what transpired a few hundred yards away, one wonders if the culprits will be found.

Sherwood was not rebuilt, and the town eventually became private property. I visited the site after attaining permission from the current owners, and it still has an eerie feel. In the springtime, one can see the lines of irises, and other bulb plants sprout and bloom in neat tidy lines, outlining where homes stood 150 years ago (they are now shielded by timber). The cemetery is overgrown and neglected, and the writing on many of the tombstones is worn and illegible, or the stones themselves are broken and sinking into the ground.

While standing near some of the oldest tombstones, I heard a man's voice. After turning to confirm that no one was there, I continued searching the tombstones. One stone in particular is interesting in that it has only a roughly carved symbol, what appears to be an L shape. In the late 1880s, a farmer who owned the land surrounding the cemetery observed an old man driving there in a rickety one-horse carriage. The man placed the unmarked boulder amongst the carved granite and limestone tombstones. It could be assumed that he was marking a grave from years before or perhaps preparing his own grave. The farmer watched the old man over several months strain with a hammer and chisel as he struggled to carve the stone. At times, the man would break down crying. He eventually stopped coming to the cemetery, and no funeral occurred. It is unknown who, if anyone, is buried in that grave, but stories began to circulate that Thomas Livingston was buried there and that the symbol was, in fact, an L for "Livingston." According to a local legend, some of Livingston's men would meet at the grave in the old Sherwood Cemetery to pay their respects to their old leader. This is an interesting detail because legend also says that his men would gather secretly at Livingston's unmarked grave in Stockton at night. Such an act would have been dangerous for some years after the war in Stockton. If Tom

Webb was able to retrieve Livingston's body from Stockton, the Sherwood Cemetery would have been an ideal final resting place, as it was secluded and surrounded by people who were supporters in life and who may have served as protectors in death.

There are stories of hauntings around the area where Sherwood once stood. Could it be spirits of residents longing for their homes or perhaps Thomas Livingston and his men? Could it be the souls of those who were not properly laid to rest at Rader Farm and stuck in a mass grave?

I can give a firsthand account of what it is like on a dark night in a place like old Sherwood. I grew up on a farm a short distance away, where there were at least three Civil War clashes, including one that was a six-day running battle, which allegedly resulted in an unmarked mass grave of thirteen dead Confederate guerrilla fighters. "Shadow people" have been observed by some people, as well as "light people," who are very much like shadow people except that they have a white luminescent appearance. A man in mid-nineteenth-century clothing has been seen there as well. But what is most interesting is the area where the skirmishes took place. I've camped there various times, and it is heavily wooded, very secluded and quiet, probably not that much different than it appeared 150 years ago during the Civil War. Everything appears normal by day.

Civil War soldiers still linger in places around Joplin, Missouri. Soldiers buried in unmarked graves may account for paranormal activity in some locations. *Reenactment photo. Courtesy of Paranormal Science Lab.*

We take our dog, a boxer, with us when we go camping up there. She is very relaxed and comfortable there until the sun goes down. We set up camp in a clearing, with the tree line a few yards beyond the ring of our campfire. Once darkness falls, our dog becomes very guarded, which is unusual for her. She becomes vigilant and, before long, acts as if she sees or hears something in the trees. But instead of running after whatever it is that she has spied as she normally would, she remains standing and begins to growl. She refuses to leave the area lit by the fire.

Later, after everyone has fallen asleep, the sound of men running through the undergrowth—lots of men, seemingly going in multiple directions at once—can be heard. At first, you assure yourself that it must be a deer, coyote or other wild animal. But it's obvious from the sheer number of running footsteps that it isn't any animal and that whatever is running is standing upright. As you lie there listening, you realize that all other noises of the area have gone silent: there are no crickets, tree frogs or any other familiar sound of a summer night.

When this occurs, our dog huddles up close to us. It seems as if all of nature collectively holds its breath, waiting for the ghostly soldiers to pass on by. I grew to anticipate these remnants of a long-lost day 150 years ago, and every time we go camping, I find myself falling asleep to the sound of their boots crunching twigs and leaves underfoot.

Joplin probably owes a bit of its existence to the fact that Sherwood was burned during the war. Sherwood was on the northern edge of present-day Joplin and the largest commercial center in the county. Moreover, mining operations were already producing sizable amounts of lead very close to Sherwood. Had it survived, Sherwood may well have expanded south to encompass what is now Joplin.

CHAPTER THREE
HAUNTED DOWNTOWN
MOBS AND LYNCHINGS

Although lead was discovered on John Cox's land around 1850, it wasn't until after the Civil War that full-scale mining operations began within the current city limits of Joplin. Eventually, hundreds of mine shafts would be sunk between Carthage to the east; Galena, Kansas, just to the west; and Picher, Oklahoma, to the southwest.

John Cox changed the name of Blytheville to Joplin in 1871, renaming the town for a minister who had lived in the Blytheville area. Pat Murphy of Carthage, Missouri, also saw the promise of the area and quickly founded Murphysburg, which was situated to the west of Cox's town and Joplin Creek (now called Turkey Creek, which runs through present-day Landreth Park). The valley in between marked the territorial division between Joplin and Murphysburg.

At one time, the area that is now Landreth Park was actively mined, and the poorest residents lived huddled in squatter shacks along its western edge, including where the old Union depot station now sits, in an area called Kansas City Flats. By late 1871, the two new cities had changed their names again, this time to East Joplin and West Joplin. There was a fierce rivalry between the two cities, which often erupted in violence as gangs of men from each side gathered in the valley along Joplin Creek.

In 1873, East and West Joplin were consolidated into one city, but this did little to stop the territorial rivalries. There are many accounts of haunted houses and paranormal activity in the area along north Main Street and the older neighborhoods just to the east of Landreth Park, including stories

 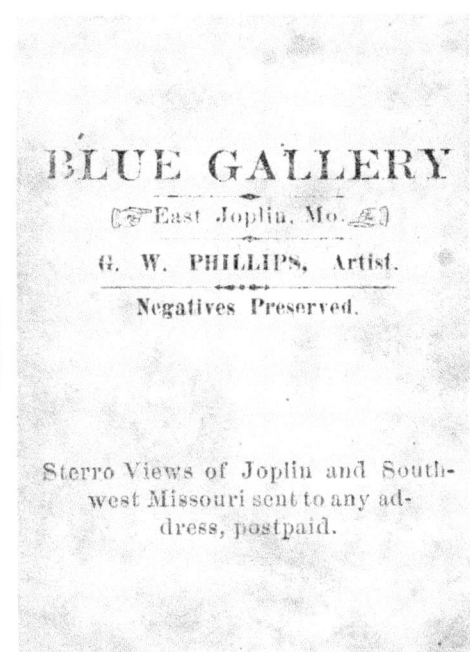

Above, left: Carte de visite photograph taken of a man at a photography studio in East Joplin, which dates the photograph to 1871–73, when Joplin was split into east and west. *Courtesy of the author.*

Above, right: Reverse side of the carte de visite photograph. *Courtesy of the author.*

Opposite, top: This vintage postcard of the Center Creek Mines in the Joplin Mining District shows piles of "chat" (or gravel) removed from mine shafts. *Courtesy of the author.*

Opposite, middle: Bitter rivalries between East and West Joplin would erupt into violence. *Reenactment photo. Courtesy of Paranormal Science Lab.*

Opposite, bottom: The confrontations between gangs of men between East and West Joplin, even after the consolidation of the two cities, too often led to death. *Reenactment photo. Courtesy of Paranormal Science Lab.*

of apparitions, poltergeist activity (such as doors closing by themselves and objects falling off shelves), voices, footsteps and so forth. Some of these are in houses that are known to have been built on the site of older homes. During the second half of the nineteenth century, the area along north Main Street was also the home to opium parlors, brothels and other less than reputable establishments. Many of these stories are difficult to confirm, and what is even more difficult is verifying the history of a particular location and its connection to paranormal activity. The number of stories that have come out of this small area indicates that there may be a higher than normal concentration of paranormal activity.

Racial tension also simmered at the time surrounding the East and West Joplin rivalries, contributing to the violence of the period. Leftover feelings from the Civil War era that led to the mutilation of black soldiers' bodies at Rader Farm flared again almost exactly forty years later. The population of African Americans increased as the general population swelled in the new mining town. In 1880, there were 7,038 residents, and of those, 246 were African American. By 1910, Joplin's population was 26,023, 773 of whom were African American. Mining was segregated in the area, and virtually no African Americans worked in the mines. Other well-paying industries were segregated as well. On April 2, 1903, the Freeman Foundry faced a worker strike because 70 white workers protested J.W. Freeman hiring Sidney Martin, a black man. A spokesman for the workers told the *Joplin Globe*, "While they would not raise such strenuous objections to the one colored man, they believe that if one is allowed to work here it will be but a short time until more are employed, and they want it understood right in

Today, this area is part of Landreth Park, but in the early days of Joplin, this area had active mines, and the poorest residents lived in shanties across this valley, collectively referred to as the Kansas City Flats. *Courtesy of the author.*

the beginning that colored men are not wanted." To avoid a strike, Freeman relented and let Martin go. As a result, blacks generally worked in service or in unskilled labor jobs. Racial tension escalated to murder and mob violence in two short weeks.

A byproduct of the mining industry was that miners tended to compensate for the rough work by spending much of their paychecks in the many saloons in town. Violence often accompanied the flow of alcohol. Such was the case on April 16, 1903, when a mob lynched a young black man named Thomas Gilyard on the streets of Joplin. It was not the first time the citizens had resorted to lynching. In 1885, a mob lynched a white man, Joe Thornton, who had killed a police officer, Daniel Sheehan. In 1900, a mob tried to lynch a black man, Leonard Barnett, who was accused of raping a white girl, but he was moved out of town before the mob accomplished its goal.

On April 15, 1903, Sam Bullock, a hardware merchant, reported to the police that two pistols had been stolen from his store, and he suspected two "colored men" were the culprits. A black man who said he knew where these men were now located accompanied Bullock to the police station. The two men and an officer named Ben May headed to the Kansas City Southern Rail Yard in north Joplin, where the witness said the thieves were hiding. Soon, Officer Theodore Leslie was sent to join the search. Leslie approached a black man standing inside a stock car and patted him down. Gunshots rang out from within the railcar, and Leslie returned fire. However, Leslie fell to the ground, having been hit in the chest and through the eye. Bystanders who witnessed the gunfire chased the suspect, a black man, as he fled on foot, and a seventeen-year-old man, Ike Clark, fired his gun at the assailant and wounded him, but the black man escaped. An all-out manhunt ensued, and police officers from nearby towns soon joined the pursuit. The *Joplin Globe* offered a $100 reward for the capture of the killer, and the reward soon grew to $1,650. The next day, the suspected killer was apprehended by two workers at the Bauer Brothers slaughterhouse after they had managed to wrestle the man's gun from him. As the two men took the suspect to the police station, he admitted to them that he had been in the railcar when Leslie was shot but that there were three other men in there and that he did not fire at the officer.

Once at the jail, a crowd started to gather and demand immediate punishment. As a precaution, the saloons were ordered closed for two hours, but this just meant that angry men had nowhere to congregate, and the crowd outside the jail grew even larger. Someone in the crowd yelled, "Break the jail down!" and several men appeared with a ten-foot-long battering ram and started pummeling the brick wall of the jail. Police officers confiscated the battering ram, but it was soon replaced by another. After ten minutes, the mob had breached the jail wall. The mob busted the lock on Gilyard's cell door with a sledgehammer and dragged him outside into the street. The jail stood on the northeast corner of Joplin Avenue and Second Street, which is now a parking lot. The mob, which had grown to an estimated three thousand men, women and children, dragged Gilyard down the street to Wall and Second Streets, not far from where the Greyhound bus station sits today. Several city officials had tried to stop the mob before it broke into the jail, but to no avail. As the mob was trying to throw a rope over a cross arm of a telephone pole, Perl Decker, the city attorney, rode through the crowd on horseback with Ike Clark. Clark yelled at the crowd that Gilyard was not the man he shot, and he definitely wasn't the man he saw kill Officer Leslie. The rope was now around Gilyard's neck, and Dr. Jesse May attempted to cut the rope with his knife, while men in the mob tried to hoist Gilyard aloft with the other end of the rope. Mayor Trigg and Mayor-elect Tom Cunningham also tried to cut the rope until forced to stop at gunpoint. A few other unnamed men tried to pull the rope back to keep Gilyard from being hoisted off his feet.

The *Joplin Daily News Herald* reported that Gilyard cried out, "Oh, God don't!" and then pleaded with the mob: "Lor' God knows dat I am innocent. Gemmen, I's got a father an' a mother. Please, foah de luhb o' massey, send foah my poor old mother before you kill me." The men who were trying to stop the lynching were driven off, and Gilyard was hoisted aloft. "A metal spike on the pole hit Gilyard's head, but he did not respond if he felt any pain. His eyes closed, his jaw fell slack. Thomas Gilyard was dead," reported the *Joplin Herald*. It was 5:50 p.m.

By 8:00 p.m., a group of men had gathered and marched up Main Street, demanding that all blacks leave Joplin. The police were unable to disperse the crowd. City officials appealed to businesses and citizens to intervene, but again to no avail. The crowd then focused on businesses that employed blacks, targeting the Imperial Barbershop first, which employed black men as barbers. Officer Ben May was able to slow the crowd and allow the black barbers time to escape out the back. The crowd was disappointed to find there were no blacks in the shop and moved on to begin a new round of violence. A white man who went by "Hickory Bill" was arrested for disturbing the peace and for firing his gun. He was taken to the jail. When the mob realized this had happened, it once again marched on the jail, demanding Hickory Bill be released. The police refused to meet the mob's demand, and the

HAUNTED JOPLIN

The far telephone pole in front of this brick building marks the approximate spot where Thomas Gilyard was lynched by a mob of three thousand in 1903 over the killing of Joplin police officer Theodore Leslie. *Courtesy of the author.*

mob then threatened to dynamite the jail. After a standoff, officers realized they were outnumbered and that the mob would not be dissuaded, so they released Hickory Bill. This did not calm the mob, as Kimberly Harper describes in *White Man's Heaven: The Lynching and Expulsion of Blacks in the Southern Ozarks, 1884–1909*, citing an article from the *Joplin Daily News Herald*:

> *The angry mob continued to grow in size as it roamed Joplin's downtown. Between Broadway and A Streets, the mob threw rocks and other objects, "at houses, through windows and at fleeing negroes." The aim of the crowd was apparently good, as a reporter observed, "There is scarcely a whole window pane in a window" on either street. The crowd managed to overturn one house before it moved on. The mob fired pistols into the air as they boldly paraded unchallenged in the night air…The crack of rifles and bursts of pistol fire were accompanied by the sound of glass breaking. Curiously, a quartet of young men followed the mob, singing songs that lightened the mood…The horde of rioters swept past Fifth and Main Streets, headed for the black section of town located at the north end of Main Street…Some of Joplin's black residents had already fled earlier that day. The blacks who were chased from Pierce City* [a few months earlier] *undoubtedly knew they were about to be*

caught up in another explosion of racial violence. They wisely fled before the mob called on them. Callers from Webb City and Galena phoned to let Joplin officials know that both cities had been inundated by a flood of black refugees, "as soon as possible after the mob began to form to hang the murderer of Theodore Leslie." Bob Carter was one of the first to leave shortly after the lynching. Carter told a reporter he left because the lynching brought back, "disagreeable memories" of a time when, "owing to a little unpleasantness some citizens of Granby [Missouri] *forced him to stretch a new rope for several minutes about two years ago…'Ah jes took one look at* [Gilyard]…*when he went up in de aiah, cause I wanted to see how I looked once an' den I went home. Ah had my turn already.' The mob torched six homes…* [and] *returned to East Seventh Street, another black area in Joplin, and set more houses on fire. At one of the fires, the firemen were unable to do much good. As fast as a line of hose was strung the mob stuck knives in it…As the mob ran rampant, though, Joplin's streets filled with blacks too scared to wait on trains to take them to safety…Ike Beechum, a black resident of Carthage, told the* [Carthage Press] *reporter that his nephew was among those who fled Joplin at the last minute. When asked if his nephew arrived in Carthage by train from Joplin, Beechum replied, "Lord, no, he beat the cars—he came over on foot."*

A small number of officials and citizens attempted to stop the mob from lynching Thomas Gilyard. *Reenactment photo. Courtesy of Paranormal Science Lab.*

To the city's credit, even as the mob was vandalizing homes and setting fires, five hundred volunteers were quickly assembled to prevent further mob violence. A coroner's inquest was called two days later, and Gilyard's body was examined. He had suffered a gunshot wound to the leg, and the bullet had lodged near his spine. The autopsy report concluded the gunshot wound was consistent with Officer Leslie shooting at someone who was standing above him inside the rail car. Ike Clark changed his story and testified that he believed Gilyard was the man he had chased after Leslie was killed. Gilyard, it turned out, was a transient from Mississippi, hopping the rail on his way to Asbury, Missouri, to join a railroad work gang. Three men were arrested for the lynching, including Hickory Bill. Sam Mitchell, one of the men charged in connection with the lynching, was identified as the man who secured the rope and climbed the telephone pole to throw it over the cross arm. He was convicted by an all-white jury and sentenced to ten years in prison. A new trial was granted based on motions filed by his attorney after trial. In the second trial, the jury did not convict him. There is speculation the reason for the jury acquitting him was that should he have been found guilty, then potentially every man, woman and child who participated in the mob would be held responsible. The court records for Hickory Bill and the third defendant have been lost, but it appears that they were not convicted (or possibly the charges were dismissed after Mitchell was acquitted).

This ugly episode in Joplin's history may also account for some of the various ghost stories that originate from the north end of downtown Joplin. The brick building that now stands next to the telephone pole is said to be haunted. I knew someone who worked in the area at night while in college, and he described it as having an eerie feel at times, that people who were in or near the building had the sensation that they were being watched. Does tension build in the atmosphere there as it did on that fateful day? Perhaps Thomas Gilyard still lingers, pondering the events of April 15 and 16, 1903, which fell a mere month before the fortieth anniversary of the Rader Farm Massacre and the burning of Sherwood.

It is not just the more common homes and buildings that experience ghostly behavior in this part of town. There are beautiful homes that were built in the late nineteenth and early twentieth centuries that have also been reported to emit this eerie feeling. One building that I am familiar with was built by a businessman who owned an implement store in Joplin in the 1890s. It is a pretty Victorian home and has been converted for apartments. The unusual activity is mainly observed in the upstairs apartments. Tenants have described similar experiences over the course of time. I was asked to do a

Left: Magnificent homes like this one line streets in the historic district in downtown Joplin, Missouri, and were built from fortunes made from the mining district. *Courtesy of the author.*

Below: These mansions demonstrate the ability of men to amass self-made fortunes in the early mining fields surrounding Joplin, Missouri. *Courtesy of the author.*

walkthrough and give an opinion as to whether the activity was paranormal in nature. When I entered the house, the batteries in my camera drained, though I had placed fresh batteries in it the evening before. I discovered this fact before I had the chance to snap any photos. I replaced the batteries with another fresh set and was able to shoot about thirty still photos before the new set of batteries drained.

As we walked upstairs, I was holding a K-II EMF meter, and the EMF (electromagnetic field) level spiked dramatically halfway up the stairs. I tested the EMF levels along the wall and near the hanging light fixture. The spike wasn't from the wiring. As we reached the landing, the owner opened the first door to our right. It opened into a single bedroom sometimes rented as a sleeping room. The owner explained that she did not use the room for anything and thought it strange how it was set up. The door locked on the outside, and there were round holes about an inch and a half wide that were drilled into the center of the wooden door in a horizontal line. The owner paused and asked if I could answer a question. She lowered her voice even though we were alone and asked, "Did they ever used to lock people up in rooms like this back then? That's what it seems since it locks on the outside." I explained that in the days before there was effective treatment for mental illness, families were left to care for their loved ones who were mentally ill. It was not uncommon for someone to be locked in a room out of sight as a way of hiding them or even as a way to prevent them from causing harm to themselves or others.

It appeared that the holes in the door had been drilled a very long time ago, and the hardware on the door looked as if it had been undisturbed for a very long time as well. I told the owner that this room may have been used for that purpose but added that we could not really reach that conclusion without more evidence. The owner shared with me the accounts given by residents, which included a sense of being watched, a feeling of uneasiness and hearing unexplained noises. Some people even refused to stay upstairs after living there for a while. I did a general sweep for EMF readings and found nothing out of the normal range. I did feel a general sense of heaviness upstairs that I had not noticed downstairs, so I could see why people might become uncomfortable if that sensation was a common occurrence. Whether that sensation or the other experiences described were connected to the sleeping room and anything in the past remains to be seen. This situation is a good example of why multiple paranormal investigations are useful in ascertaining the nature of unexplained activity in a location and connecting it to past events.

The John Wise House is another house in the historic downtown area that is reported to have paranormal activity, but I haven't observed any activity personally. John Wise moved to Joplin in 1874 to open a hide and grain business. He quickly realized that money could be made in mining and soon joined forces with Thomas Connor to operate lead mines. He also owned three thousand acres of land in Oklahoma, where he invested in coal mining and cattle and horse ranching. Wise helped organize a miner's bank and served on the city council. In 1898, he commissioned a fanciful Queen Anne–style house. Built for $10,000, the home featured round towers, balconies and stained-glass windows. In 1920, Mrs. Wise convinced her husband that their house would make a good residential facility for the YWCA. Although the YMCA had a fine building on east Fourth Street, the women's organization had yet to find a suitable home. Instead, it shuffled between various old houses and vacant upper floors in downtown buildings. In 1920, a group of businessmen raised funds to purchase the Wise house for $15,000 and spent another $13,000 to remodel and furnish it. The new YWCA opened as a boardinghouse for girls who came to Joplin to work. The facility lodged up to forty girls. The young women had to walk a few blocks to eat their meals at the YWCA cafeteria at 514½ Joplin Street.

The John Wise House. Do events from its past as a private home, YWCA boarding home and a bed-and-breakfast replay within these walls? *Courtesy of the author.*

The house later passed back to private hands and, in recent years, was turned into the John Wise Bed and Breakfast Inn. It has recently been sold and turned into an apartment building. I have been told by multiple people that disembodied voices and footsteps have been heard. This is not unusual for a house that has been lived in by a lot of people. Reports I have heard would tend to make a better case for residual activity rather than interactive, as it does not sound as if there is a presence aware of the living people there. This is similar to walking into a house for the first time and feeling welcomed and positive for no particular reason. The happiness experienced in the house over time seems to have an impact on the house itself. Residual paranormal activity is much the same, where the people who have been there in the past left an impression on the environment. Likewise, it is not clear whether the paranormal activity is a result of its use as a private residence or YWCA or if it is from another cause.

CHAPTER FOUR

PROSPERITY SCHOOL BED AND BREAKFAST

REFUSING TO FADE AWAY

Prosperity began as a lead and zinc mining camp six miles east of Joplin. The Troup Mining Company was opened in 1888 and was located on forty acres of land that eventually became known as Prosperity. Among its main investors was Curtis Wright, a furniture maker from Connersville, Indiana. Apparently, he set out to Missouri in order to seek a new challenge. Wright was also an amateur geologist and came to the Joplin Mining District to indulge that interest. He liked what he saw and wrote home, promising his wife that if she would agree to the move, he would build her the biggest house in Carthage, Missouri. He added that he planned to invest in the lead and zinc mines but intended to make his new career in the limestone quarries of the area. True to his word, Curtis Wright built a magnificent Queen Anne–style home for his wife, Nira, and also became involved in the limestone industry, operating the Carthage Stone Company and other related companies. His home, formerly located at 304 West Macon, was built in 1891 and was constructed of local limestone and timber. Wright placed rock from his mines on the façades of the eaves.

So began Prosperity, Missouri, located at the end of a branch of the Southwest Missouri Electric Railroad and on a spur of the Missouri Pacific Railroad. By 1899, more than twenty mines were in operation, and a population of over 1,500 made Prosperity much more than a mining camp. In 1907, Tom Tarrant and his brothers built the Prosperity School from local Carthage stone and red and yellow bricks to serve the swelling numbers of families with children. Like most schools of the time period, it served all grades. During its heyday, Prosperity had a bank, stores and other businesses. The Joplin-area mining district experienced a decline with dropping lead prices during the late 1920s. There was an increase in demand during World War II, then the final decline after the war as cheaper sources were developed overseas. This marked the beginning of the migration from the town of Prosperity. The school held on and operated until 1962, when it had about thirty students left. Now all that remains of the once prosperous town is the school building and a few homes.

After the school closed down, the building stood empty for more than thirty years, until the current owners, Richard and Janet Roberts, purchased it in 1994 and renovated the building, keeping the architecture very much the same as when it functioned as a schoolhouse. The building reopened as the Prosperity School Bed and Breakfast Inn in 2000. The school gained a reputation over the years as being haunted, and teenagers would often enter it in the dead of night. Rumors of it being haunted continued even after the building became a bed-and-breakfast. I have spoken to people who attended Prosperity School as children, and some are very hostile to the notion that

The Prosperity School Bed and Breakfast Inn combines the charm of the old schoolhouse with the elegance of a lovely inn. Some guests encounter more company than others during their stay. *Courtesy of the author.*

the building is haunted, feeling that it gives the school a negative image. On the other hand, its reputation for being haunted has drawn visitors to stay the night. However, from the perspective of a paranormal investigator, it raises the issue of how the stories of paranormal activity originated. Having grown up within a few miles of the Prosperity School, I can say I have heard stories since my childhood of it being a scary place that some people considered haunted, but many abandoned buildings hold that reputation. I had not heard detailed firsthand accounts that would give these stories authenticity, so I was unsure if these stories were merely made up by teenagers who had scared themselves in an empty building. Additionally, it has become a destination for paranormal investigators, including The Atlantic Paranormal Society (TAPS) of the television show *Ghost Hunters*. Video footage of what the videographer claims to be the ghosts of young children running down a hall has appeared on the Internet. The video was impressive on first viewing, but it is hard to judge from the camera angle whether these shadows could be cast by people running down the hallway, as the camera was in a cross hallway and only a narrow field of vision can be seen in the video footage. Needless to say, I was definitely curious to find out for myself when PSL had the opportunity to conduct an investigation at the Prosperity School Bed and Breakfast Inn.

The inn is a wonderful mix of the former school and a lovely bed-and-breakfast. It is very nicely decorated and homey, yet it retains the charm of a schoolhouse, including the coatroom next to the restrooms, the former stage incorporated into one of the guest suites and the original bell tower above. Four members of PSL arrived on a sunny afternoon to meet the owners and to conduct an initial walkthrough of the inn. The Robertses are gracious and enjoyable hosts. The inn displays many items documenting the school's past, providing many potential "trigger objects"—items that may have a meaning to any ghosts or entities in a location that could trigger paranormal activity.

The current dining room and the parlor directly beside it are separated by a large archway. These rooms are said to have paranormal activity, including the sounds of school desks and chairs being scooted across the floor and footsteps, perhaps from students or maybe a janitor cleaning at the end of the day. The centerpiece of the dining room is a large, ornate dark walnut dining table with a glossy finish. We were shown small fingerprints on the table, which appear to be set in the finish, as if children touched the surface while the lacquer was still damp. The owners attest that the fingerprints were not always present. According to the Robertses, they

The ornate dining table with mysterious fingerprints that do not wipe away at the Prosperity School Bed and Breakfast Inn as viewed from the adjoining parlor. The doorway where the shadow person was seen is on the far right side of the frame. *Courtesy of Paranormal Science Lab.*

were seated around the table one evening with a paranormal investigator they are acquainted with, and when they got up to investigate something they heard, they returned to find the fingerprints there. They attempted to wipe the prints off with polish but to no avail.

It was at this point in PSL's tour that a shadow person revealed itself. A shadow person is not an apparition in the traditional sense, like a ghost that appears as a fully formed human being. Instead, it appears as a shadow with a human outline but no discernible details. Shadow people do not cast a shadow on the floor or wall as a living person or other solid object would. While we were in the dining room and parlor area talking with the Robertses, I happened to be standing in the corner of the dining room, diagonal from the door to the main hallway. As I was standing there, contemplating whether the fingerprints were made when the finish was still wet, I watched a shadow person come to the doorway, lean forward as if looking into the room very quickly and then rush past the open doorway. It was a bright sunny day, and the hallway was well lit. Everyone was in the dining room and parlor, so no living person could have caused the shadow. It was approximately four feet tall. Unfortunately, since we were on an initial walkthrough, no cameras were set up. However, my seeing the shadow figure indicated that there was a chance that paranormal activity could be documented there. Our investigation occurred on a warm early summer night with clear skies and no breeze. The area is rural, with very little noise contamination from the road or surrounding area.

One story that is circulated as a possible cause for any haunting at the Prosperity School Bed and Breakfast Inn is a tale of a teacher and a mother of a student arguing upstairs. As the story goes, during the confrontation, the little girl was somehow accidentally bumped into, and she lost her balance and fell out of a second-story window. This story has not been confirmed as true. Another ghost story involves an antique cabinet with doors and shelves in the upstairs hall that leads to one of the suites. The owners state that guests have reported seeing a nurse dressed in an early twentieth-century uniform standing in front of the cabinet with her hand extended, as if picking up bottles or jars off shelves and looking at them. Now the cabinet is full of linens and towels, but the cabinet was found in the basement of the building, so it is possible that it was a supply closet for the school nurse at some point in time.

Three of the four guest suites are named for longtime teachers at the school. Miss Pink Saxton's Room is decorated in shades of pink and burgundy and has an antique brass bed with a private bath featuring a claw-foot tub with a hand-held showerhead. Miss Rose Saxton's Room is cast in shades of green and has a four-poster canopy bed and plenty of roses. Miss Pansy Smith's Room features a high-back Victorian bed, a New Orleans armoire and walls covered in pansies that are snuggled amidst amethyst tones. The Prosperity Suite rounds out the choice of suites with an elegant high-back bed and matching décor. There are more intriguing stories that have come from guests of the inn.

Rose's room is the site of multiple phenomena. Guests have been awakened by the sensation of a small child crawling into the bed beside them, even feeling tugs on the blankets. One woman who was staying in the room by herself said that she was awakened by this sensation but, in her drowsiness, thought it was one of her children and fell back to sleep only to awaken the next morning to the realization that it could not have been one of her children as they were not with her. Rose's room is also known to play havoc with electronic equipment, including cameras. We experienced this situation with our cameras during our investigation. Three cameras were set up, recording to a digital video recorder. On multiple occasions during the investigation, an area of distortion would appear on video, almost like heat radiating off hot asphalt during the summer. However, the area of distortion would move about the room. If an investigator was in the room when the distortion appeared, the distortion tended to move toward the person and appeared to distort the image of the person as if it was something with mass and was situated between the person and the camera. We attempted to find a natural explanation for this distortion but without result. There were no strong EMF fields or unusual lighting or other conditions identified that

Staircase in the Prosperity School Bed and Breakfast Inn. The white on the left side of the frame is a moth, and on close inspection, the shape of the wings is visible. *Courtesy of Paranormal Science Lab.*

could have affected the quality of the video. The cameras were changed out with other cameras to verify that the cameras had not developed a malfunction, but the replacements experienced the same distortion. We were informed by the owners that similar activity had been observed by other paranormal investigators.

Pansy's room includes a Jacuzzi-style bathtub. We were informed that, on occasion, the motor that runs the water jets turns on by itself and runs. The owners said that this started not long after it was installed, and the manufacturer has attempted to find the cause for this apparent defect but found the tub in perfect working order. Likewise, no defect in the wiring was found. The cause for this unusual activity is unexplained. The bathtub remained silent while we were present.

At the end of the second floor, near the staircase, is an open area where an antique table sits under a window. The owners informed us that one evening, during an EVP session around that table, questions were being asked about any Civil War activity on the grounds. An EVP was captured naming a doctor. After some research, Mrs. Roberts said she was able to confirm that there was a doctor so named who served in the Civil War and was part of a unit from Indiana. While this may seem a mere coincidence, it cannot be dismissed without further review. A number of units from other states, including Indiana, fought within the state of Missouri. While it has not been confirmed that this doctor was in the Prosperity area during the Civil War, it is possible, as records of units were far from complete, especially here in the western theater. One seemingly mundane fact contributed to the incomplete unit records: the scarcity of paper needed to write the reports. In truth, there may well have been a skirmish on the grounds surrounding Prosperity School, as southwest Missouri saw some of the most intense guerrilla warfare in the Civil War. It is estimated that up to one thousand partisan rangers operated in southwest Missouri at any given time during the war. Many skirmishes and incidents of violence in this area are lost to history. Stories of sightings of Civil War soldiers' ghosts in locations not known to have experienced Civil War violence are not uncommon.

Pink's room was the center of activity during our investigation. Cold spots with temperature drops documented by thermometers were detected and could not be explained by any draft or air conditioning. Such cold spots are often associated with paranormal activity. The theory is that entities draw energy from the atmosphere in order to interact and manifest, and due to the energy exchange, there is a drop in temperature. EVP sessions were conducted multiple times during the night with surprisingly consistent responses. These responses indicated that the spirit of a woman who was a teacher at the school was present. During some of the EVP sessions, multiple flashlights were used as objects for an entity to interact with investigators. Questions were asked, requesting that the entity turn on a light if the response was yes and not turn on a light if the response was no. In other sessions, questions were asked, requesting that the entity turn on a blue flashlight if the response was yes or to turn on a red flashlight if the response was no. The responses using both methods were consistent. The responses indicated that the teacher, Rose Saxton, was present and that she was not sad or lonely.

While sitting on the bottom stair, an EVP session was conducted, and it produced two interesting EVPs of a male voice. The first EVP was about

Pink's room in the Prosperity School Bed and Breakfast Inn while an EVP session is being conducted. *Courtesy of Paranormal Science Lab.*

The Prosperity School has weathered more than a century and survived the community it was named after. It stands as a solemn reminder of the working men who made this area a prosperous mining industry. *Courtesy of the author.*

forty-five seconds into the session. After asking if anyone there liked the owners, the audio recorder captured an EVP of a man's voice replying, "In charge." About twenty-five seconds later, an investigator asked the question "Where are you at?" and the same voice replied, "Right behind."

We set up cameras in three directions, trying to duplicate the Internet video showing shadows of children running down the hallway upstairs. We placed them at both ends of the hallway facing each other and also placed a camera in the intersecting hallway in the same position as the camera in the video. Unfortunately, no anomalies were captured in the hallway. As such, no conclusion can be made about the video of the running shadows. The video does make an impression, though, but without seeing video from the ends of the hallway, there is no way of objectively evaluating the cause of the shadows.

There do appear to be anomalies present at the Prosperity School Bed and Breakfast Inn. Are there former students running the halls, teachers still leading classes or other employees such as a nurse or janitor going about their routines as they did in life? Could there be Civil War soldiers or perhaps miners who died in the immediate area also occupying space within the old schoolhouse? I know I saw a shadow move down the hallway in broad daylight without a satisfactory explanation, although we could not count the experience as evidence since it was not captured on camera. EVPs and strange distortions that moved around in the camera frame were captured. There does appear to be paranormal activity, but the exact nature is yet to be determined. Regardless, a night in the Prosperity School Bed and Breakfast Inn, whether as a paranormal investigator or a guest, will leave memories unlikely to fade quickly.

CHAPTER FIVE
The Stefflebeck Bordello
HOUSE OF HORRORS

Today, as you drive through Galena, Kansas, it is hard to imagine this small town of three thousand having ten times that number in population, but that was the case in the 1890s. Of the thirty thousand people, many were single men busily seeking their fortunes in the booming lead and zinc mining fields in and around Galena, just west of Joplin. But don't make the mistake of assuming that everyone in the mining fields made their fortune by descending into the mine shafts. Many entrepreneurs figured out that in the Joplin mining district, as well as mining towns across the western United States, there was more money to be made from providing goods and services to the miners than trying your hand at mining yourself. However, few were as crafty or coldblooded as Ma Stefflebeck. Her real name was Nancy Stefflebeck or, by some accounts, Mrs. Charles Wilson.

In the 1890s, the atmosphere was no less rough in Galena than it was in Joplin. At this time, the sprawling cities expanded rapidly until their outskirts merged, making it difficult to define where one ended and the other began as you went down the road. As in Joplin, the favorite pastime of miners in Galena was spending their paycheck in the saloons, gambling parlors and bawdyhouses. The north portion of Main Street in Galena was known for its houses of ill repute, and the area itself was called the red-light zone. With more than thirty thousand miners in town, most of whom were not from the area, it is not surprising that crime was rampant, and it was not unusual for an intoxicated miner to disappear after an argument at the poker table.

The Stefflebeck Bordello as it appears today. Ma Stefflebeck's fortune may still lay buried somewhere nearby. *Courtesy of the author.*

Ma Stefflebeck was, at heart, an opportunist, and she set out to make money off of the miners. She opened a bordello at the corner of Main and Fort Streets in the red-light zone. The Stefflebeck Bordello was a very popular and busy place, and Ma Stefflebeck reportedly became a wealthy woman in a few years. Though Ma Stefflebeck chafed at the amount of money that was displayed in her house, she wasn't able to entice the miners to spend at her establishment.

One evening, Stefflebeck studied a miner who was buying one drink after another and noticed that he was paying for those drinks with gold coins that he kept in a leather pouch secured to his belt. Figuring from the size of the bag that it contained several hundred dollars, she began to calculate a plan. She waited until the man was very drunk and enticed him into one of the backrooms. Instead of the entertainment he had been expecting, the unfortunate man was greeted by one of Stefflebeck's sons who attacked him with an axe, splitting the miner's head open. Later, the body was concealed in a canvas bag or feed sack and removed from the house under cover of darkness in a buggy. The body was disposed of in one of the abandoned mine shafts in the area.

Ma Stefflebeck didn't stop with that murder, as it became more profitable than the bordello itself. It is speculated that Stefflebeck's two sons and her boyfriend, Charles Wilson (who by some accounts was actually her husband), assisted in the murders. She was careful to target miners who were transients, with no ties to the area. In this way, it was less likely someone would look for them too hard. Additionally, she was prudent and did not spend money extravagantly; in fact, she lived very frugally. She did not use banks and ran a cash business, so no one had any idea how much money she amassed. She avoided suspicion of the authorities for several years and was thought to have killed between thirty and fifty victims, but it is really unknown how many men succumbed to her plot.

The murders could have possibly gone on undetected for years had it not been for an argument she had with one of the prostitutes she employed. She and the girl, Cora, had a heated exchange, and Ma Stefflebeck fired the girl and told her to leave the house. The nature of the argument is unknown. In retaliation, Cora went to the police in town and informed them of the murders. Stefflebeck, her sons and Charles Wilson were arrested the next day. Police searched the bordello thoroughly but could not find any money that had been taken from the victims. When officers searched nearby abandoned mine shafts, more than a dozen bodies were found. Authorities estimated that Stefflebeck had hidden as much as $50,000 in money and jewelry stolen from the victims.

Ma Stefflebeck, Charles Wilson and her sons were tried for the murder of Frank Galbraith. All four were convicted of murder in 1897 and sent to prison. Stefflebeck never revealed where the money was hidden. She died in prison in 1909, taking the secret with her to the grave. After her death, treasure hunters flocked to Galena when the story was republished, some coming from as far away as Colorado. The house was ransacked and floorboards were pried up, but again, no stash of money was found. To this day, it is unknown where the money was hidden, whether it was in the bordello or somewhere else in the Galena area. Likewise, it is unknown if some other person with knowledge of the murders, perhaps another one of the girls working at the bordello, quietly took it on themselves to take the money.

Regardless of the fate of the stolen money, the bordello has stood empty for decades and is now boarded up. The old house has lost the luster of its former glory and sits rotting away slowly. But it, too, still holds secrets, as did Ma Stefflebeck. The current owner has plans to preserve the house, but it will be a question of whether time wins the battle. It is reputed that the ghosts of Ma Stefflebeck's victims have remained at the bordello all these years. The house currently has areas where the floors have been removed, and exploring its interior can be risky. Permission must be sought from the owner, and I advise against entry without permission. People report being touched by spirits in the bordello, a sensation described as being similar to running dry ice along your skin. There are unexplained EMF spikes, but there is no electricity in the building. Footsteps are heard where no one is walking, and various EVPs have been captured.

CHAPTER SIX
HAUNTED HOSPITALS
PAST AND PRESENT

Many sightings of ghosts and paranormal activity have been reported in hospitals, where suffering and death occur on a daily basis. The Sisters of Mercy came to Joplin in the early days of the mining operations, and even before they built a hospital, they attended to the injuries and health needs of the citizens of Joplin. In 1883, a tornado caused widespread damage to Joplin, and the Sisters of Mercy were "buffeted and blown about by the wind as they strove in vain to keep out the sheets of water thrown against the west end of the building [they were using,] which stands high and unprotected." In 1900, the Sisters of Mercy built the first hospital serving Joplin. St. John's Hospital was originally located on Sergeant Street at Twenty-second Street. In 1968, it was closed and operations were moved to the new nine-story facility on McClelland Boulevard. The site of the original hospital now contains a senior citizens' center.

The city's second hospital was located across the street and a block away from the original St. John's Hospital. Freeman's Hospital was established in 1922 when John W. Freeman donated his family home, which was located at 2008 Sergeant Street. The first Freeman Hospital was named in honor of John Freeman's late son, Orley. Three years later, a seventy-five-bed addition was added to the original home, and Freeman Hospital, staffed with nineteen nurses and five physicians and surgeons, opened its doors to patients. The hospital was added onto over the years but was closed in 1975 in favor of the new Freeman Hospital complex located on Thirty-second Street today.

The area around the site of these two early hospitals is heavy with paranormal activity, which is not restricted to the physical sites of the hospitals. I was told of the experiences of one family that lived in a home within a block of both of these old hospitals. Their small son saw things that his parents could not, and at times, these unknown things upset him, but he wasn't old enough to clearly communicate why he was upset. Occasionally, the mother and father each sensed the presence of something in the house, and objects would move on their own. One day, the boy's father saw a box of aluminum foil slide across the kitchen counter and onto the floor. Whether this activity was from past events connected with the house itself or whether it was connected to one or both of the hospitals is unknown.

The old Freeman Hospital has been known to have paranormal activity over the years. It stands dark and empty now but is reportedly not silent. The old morgue, as well as other areas, is said to have unexplained footsteps and sounds reminiscent of those that filled those rooms and corridors in years past. It is a building that conveys a foreboding feeling even from the outside. There have been various stories of people going into the building only to end up running out, frightened by what they encountered. However, the building is privately owned, and the owner does not want urban explorers or other people in the building.

The new St. John's Hospital, built in 1968, was rendered structurally unsound after the May 22, 2011 F5 tornado cut a swath through Joplin almost a mile wide and thirteen miles long. It is currently scheduled to be demolished, and a new facility will be built in another location. There were stories of ghosts in the hospital while it was still in use. Specifically, people who worked at the hospital say that there were ghosts on both the fourth and seventh floors. After the tornado, the windows were blown out and open to the elements. People started reporting seeing ghost apparitions in the building as they passed by. Whether they were seeing the same ghosts that staff had seen previously is not known. Several people died in the hospital during the tornado, including a patient who was sucked out of a window. Whether paranormal activity will remain on the site after demolition is complete is an open question, but oftentimes, activity continues even after a new building is erected on the same site.

The former Jasper County Tuberculosis Sanatorium is a site that has experienced a lot of paranormal activity over the years. It was built just after the turn of the twentieth century at Webb City. It was a large, two-story red brick building, designed in the typical three-sided U shape like

The old Freeman Hospital as it sits today. Ghosts are said to roam these empty hallways. Perhaps the specters within roam the nearby neighborhood as well. *Courtesy of the author.*

St. John's Hospital in the aftermath of the May 22, 2011 F5 tornado. This building is currently scheduled to be demolished. *Courtesy of the author.*

This rock wall is the only reminder of the Jasper County Tuberculosis Sanatorium, which later became the Elmhurst Nursing Home. The building sat about one hundred yards behind this wall. *Courtesy of the author.*

most sanatoriums from that period. The front of the building faced south, and the south side originally would have had open breezeways to utilize the natural airflow, as it was believed fresh air was good for the patients' lungs. Many patients passed away at the sanatorium. Later, the building was converted into the Elmhurst Nursing Home, which operated until the 1980s. Staff and visitors experienced various paranormal events, including hearing voices of nurses making their rounds, feeling the temperature change in cold spots, seeing unexplained movement of shadows and so forth. I have heard former employees talk about how uncomfortable it was to work nightshifts. The building was eventually torn down and replaced with a new building, which still operates as a nursing home. The new building sits a few hundred feet behind the footprint of the original building. I heard one former employee wonder whether the activity now occurs in the new building. I have also heard people who have spent time in the building as children of employees say that there were times they were frightened.

Webb City was the site of one of the first hospitals that was run by the Salvation Army. It was replaced by the Jane Chinn Hospital in 1910. When the hospital opened, it was equipped with the latest technology of the day. It was supported by the mines and miners in the district. According to a *History of Jasper County, Missouri, and Its People*,

> *Subscriptions of twenty-five cents per month are taken from the miners, and the mine operators pay five dollars per month, which is enough for the running expenses of the hospital. Miss Houser is the present superintendent of the hospital and is assisted by three nurses. There is one room in the hospital that is not used and that is the morgue, for, instead of keeping the dead at the hospital they are removed to a downtown morgue. The Chinns have made their money from Jasper county mines and the hospital is a monument to their generosity.*

The hospital closed in the 1980s. However, staff talked of a haunting well before the hospital closed its doors. Many employees felt that the operating room was haunted, and some of the janitorial staff did not like being in the operating room alone for that reason. The building sat empty, and then in the 1990s, it was used as a haunted house at Halloween for several years. Actors in the haunted house, as well as people going through the haunted house, reported paranormal activity, including footsteps and

Jane Chinn Hospital served the community for over seventy years, but it has long been the subject of tales of ghosts roaming the halls and operating room. *Courtesy of the author.*

disembodied voices. One man reported having his dog with him. The dog went to the landing between the first and second floors and began whining and barking hysterically. Others have reported the sound of a rolling gurney on the second floor in and near the operating room. Today, the building has been converted into senior apartments.

CHAPTER SEVEN
The Olivia Apartments

GRAND LIVING

The five-story, Roman-Greco Revival (also known as Pompeian fashion), red brick and stone Olivia Apartment Building was the vision of Arthur Enrico (A.E.) Bendelari. Some sources name him as Anton Bendelari, but this appears to be a mistake. No birth records or original sources identify an Anton Bendelari as being in the southwest Missouri area or involved with the business concerns in the area. It is unclear where this misnomer originated. Arthur Bendelari was a partner in the State Lead and Zinc Company and the Southwestern Machinery Company and was later president of the Eagle-Picher Lead Company, the largest mining company in the Joplin-Picher mining district. A complex man, Arthur Bendelari was a mining engineer who, among other accomplishments, was the inventor of the Bendelari Jig used in mines to separate different sizes of mineral deposits. The Bendelari Jig is still manufactured by a company in Joplin and continues to be used in mining operations around the world. Bendelari also invented and patented a design for an improved collapsible cardboard box for shipping beer bottles in 1912.

Arthur Bendelari was born in Canada in 1880 and came to Joplin in 1901 as a mine supervisor for the Underwriters Land Company. Bendelari quickly became known as a hard worker. Oliver Picher took notice of Bendelari (known as Bendi to his friends) and hired him to supervise the mining operations of Picher Lead Company (which was based in Joplin), and Bendelari served as a company agent, leasing and exploring land for lead ore in the new Picher, Oklahoma mining field. Bendelari was perhaps

L.M. Wilson mailed this vintage postcard of the Olivia Apartments to Mrs. Dewitt Franklin in Maysville, Kentucky, on August 18, 1910. Wilson marked two x's to indicate where their apartment was in the building. *Courtesy of the author.*

the foremost expert on the tri-state mining district, and he became very wealthy in a relatively short period of time.

Bendelari had a reputation for having a genteel personality and a low-key management style, which was rare in the rough-and-tumble mining district. A good example of this disposition to take things in stride led to the discovery of the largest lead and zinc field in the world at Picher, Oklahoma, as recounted by Evan Just:

> *Along about 1915, there was some evidence of lead outcroppings down in the Oklahoma area. Arthur Bendelari was sent down to do some drilling in Oklahoma. They had done this drilling, and it was a failure. This was for the [Picher Lead] Company. So the drilling rigs started on their way home to the Joplin area, and one got stuck in the mud in a rainy spell, and the driller asked if because of the extra cost of that situation, would Bendelari let him drill a hole where he was stuck. They drilled into the Picher field, which was a part of the bigger field, and eventually the most productive of all. In other words, it opened up a tremendous mining district out on the flat, prairie country where there had been almost no evidence of mineralization just because of this fortuitous circumstance that the driller got stuck in the mud.*

In 1919, when the Picher Lead Company merged with the Eagle White Lead Works, Bendelari became the director of mining operations for the new company, Eagle-Picher, which remained the largest mining company in the tri-state mining district. He continued to rise through the upper management of Eagle-Picher, and in 1928, he was named president of the company. Lead prices dropped in the late 1920s, and a year after Bendelari became president of the company, the Great Depression hit, and he moved the company's headquarters back to Cincinnati, where Eagle White Lead Works had originated in the mid-1800s. He remained in Cincinnati and later purchased a horse farm outside Lexington, Kentucky. After that point, Arthur Bendelari was removed from the Joplin area.

Bendelari built the Olivia when he was twenty-six years old, paying for it out of his own money—a staggering $150,000. The Olivia featured luxurious amenities that were not widely available in the Midwest in 1906. Bendelari named this extravagant building "Olivia" in honor of his mother.

Bendelari commissioned local architect Allen Austin to design a European-style building, where every apartment featured large, dark French doors that opened onto a private balcony. Interestingly, not one of the apartments had a kitchen, as there was a world-class chef on staff who prepared elegant cuisine in the state-of-the-art kitchen on the fifth floor. The kitchen was adjacent to the formal dining room, which is still impressive in scope and detail. The dining room featured an oak floor and six-foot-high, quarter-

Vintage postcard of Eagle-Picher's smelter operations in Galena, Kansas. *Courtesy of the author.*

sawn oak paneling and was illuminated by light from massive windows on two sides. These remain, although the floor is worn from decades of use. On opening day, light poured in the windows and was replaced by gas lights at night, each table receiving its own lamp. At that time, Joplin was still full of dirt-paved streets, and indoor lighting was not universal for the residents. Above the oak wainscot, hand-painted murals decorated the twelve-foot-high walls and the ceiling surfaces. Large oak tables and leather-upholstered oak chairs furnished the area, which totaled five thousand square feet, including the kitchen. For those who preferred less formal dining, the "grill room," also on the fifth floor, offered broiled meats. The dining rooms were open to both tenants and the public. Today, the murals are gone, but visitors still stand in awe when entering the dining room for the first time.

The fifth floor also featured a private dining room, and it is easy to imagine Bendelari and other business leaders conducting business behind closed doors. It, too, was complimented with six-foot-high oak paneling, marble baseboards and decorative painting on the ceiling. A rooftop garden allowed privileged onlookers a panoramic view of Joplin, and while the garden is gone, the rooftop still offers a breathtaking view. The basement floor housed a diner, barbershop, pool hall and more conveniences that were seldom seen in one place at the time. This allowed residents of the Olivia, as well as people in the surrounding neighborhood, to eat and attend to daily errands without traveling across the city.

On its opening day, the *Joplin Globe* described the Olivia as Bendelari's "monumental testimonial to the universal confidence in Joplin's future." The newspaper reporter who wrote the article asserted that "nothing more elegant, more stylish, more convenient has ever been erected in Joplin."

The public spaces of the Olivia are adorned with solid Italian marble. The lobby is impressive even today, and one is left imagining how the sight would have appeared in 1906.

The front entrance to the Olivia Apartment Building. Notice the detail above the doors, including the spider web motif in leaded glass. *Courtesy of the author.*

The front entrance is framed by massive wooden doors that are topped by leaded glass in a spider web design, which inspires one to ponder whether Bendelari had an interest in the macabre. There is no evidence that he did. Instead, the spider web was a common decorative motif in the Pompeian style and merely a part of the Greco-Roman Revival design. Our modern connotation of spider webs as part of all that is scary and unspoken in the dark sets the mood for the paranormal tale I am about to share.

Through the huge wooden doors, one's attention is brought to the mosaic tiles on the foyer floor that spell out "Olivia." Passing through the elaborate foyer, the lobby opens into a spacious area that evokes daydreams of old European villas lit by skylights and framed by massive Italian marble columns. A concave dome fills the ceiling, covered in wallpaper depicting a Renaissance scene. Originally, this was a skylight that would flood the area with sun- or moonlight. Unfortunately, the onlooker can now only imagine what the original centerpiece of this space—a large west-facing leaded-glass window with the name "Olivia" that was expertly crafted in multicolored glass—would have looked like. As the building experienced neglect and disrepair over the last decades, the stained-glass Olivia windowpanes (which measure approximately twelve feet in length and eight in height) disappeared and were replaced with clear pane glass. While still aesthetically pleasing, it is easy to visualize the imposing statement made by those six letters in stained glass: that this, the Olivia, is a place to be remembered.

This elegant reminder of Joplin's early days where some made incredible fortunes when luck shone on them with favor is now shrouded in silence. The Olivia operated as an apartment building for one hundred years before finally closing its doors. The building has been placed on the National Register of Historic Places, and the current owners have been working to renovate the building to its former splendor.

Arthur Bendelari married Frances Geddes, the daughter of James Irvin Geddes, who was a mining promoter in the Joplin area, an attorney and the former editor-owner of the *Joplin Herald* newspaper. The Bendelaris had their private residence on the first floor of the Olivia in what is believed to have been the southeast side of the building. The Geddeses also resided in the Olivia, and when Arthur's father-in-law passed away in 1923, his body was laid in state for public viewing at the Olivia. But James Geddes was not the first visit of death at the Olivia, nor was his the most tragic. That distinction is reserved for the night of January 12, 1908, and the unfortunate Marvin Reynolds.

The lobby of the Olivia, facing west toward the window that once held the stained-glass letters spelling out Olivia. *Courtesy of Paranormal Science Lab.*

Marvin Reynolds was a twenty-year-old night desk clerk at the Olivia. It is believed that in the early hours of January 12, 1908, while the residents slept above, Marvin went to the basement to feed the building cat (having a cat in a building was a common practice then in order to control the building's mice population). It appears that the luxurious amenities provided at the Olivia were the unintended catalyst of terror and agonizing death. The lighting throughout the building was powered by natural gas, which was not uncommon at the time and was viewed by many as more dependable than electricity. Apparently, Marvin Reynolds flipped a light switch in the darkened basement, and the light did not come on. He pulled out a match and struck it, igniting gas vapors in the air that caused a massive explosion. The massive blast and resulting shockwave threw Mr. and Mrs. John F. Stevens out of their bed in their first-floor apartment on the northeast side of the building, the same side where the boiler was located. The explosion pulverized heavy oak furniture, stripped plaster from the walls, reduced the floor to toothpicks and blew out windows of the Olivia and nearby houses. The railing of the front veranda was blown into the street. Since inspectors found no serious structural damage to the Olivia, Bendelari rebuilt as soon as possible.

Marvin Reynolds was not so lucky. It is unlikely that Marvin realized the basement had a gas leak. Natural gas is colorless and odorless. The sulfur-like smell we associate with natural gas today is due to an odorant added to warn people of a leak. However, it was not until the 1920s that odorants were commonly used in natural gas.

Very little coverage appeared in the local newspapers detailing the explosion, but there were stories carried in newspapers across the country describing the horrific destruction. However, no newspaper told the full story. The most reliable account comes from the lawsuit filed by Mr. and Mrs. John F. Stevens against their insurance carrier under their fire insurance policy. What follows is an excerpt from the decision and opinion of the Missouri Court of Appeals in the case:

123 S.W. 63
STEPHENS [sic] v FIRE ASS'N OF PHILADELPHIA
Springfield Court of Appeals. Missouri.
December 6, 1909.

Appeal from Circuit Court, Jasper County; Haywood Scott, Judge.

Action by J.E. [sic] Stephens against the Fire Association of Philadelphia. Judgment for plaintiff, and defendant appeals. Affirmed.

NIXON, Presiding Judge.

This is an action on a fire insurance policy. The petition alleges that the property insured was household furniture on the first floor just above the basement of what is known as the Olivia Apartment House, on the corner of Fourth and Moffett streets in Joplin, Mo., which furniture was damaged and destroyed by a fire and an explosion on January 12, 1908, at about 5 o'clock in the morning. The basement underneath this apartment was used for lockers and storage for tenants in the building, and it was in this basement that the fire and explosion occurred by which the contents of the building were badly wrecked and damaged, including household goods and other personal property alleged to have been worth, at a sound value, from $4,000 to $5,000...The case was tried...upon the same theory—that if the fire preceded the explosion, and the explosion was an incident of the fire and was caused by it, the insured could recover the fire damage only. The evidence tended to show...that a severe explosion happened in the building, with probabilities that it occurred from natural gas in the basement directly under the apartment occupied by the plaintiff...

The superintendent of the Kansas Natural Gas Company testified that he had been familiar with the gas business since 1887. He was asked the following questions:

Q. Will natural gas explode unless it comes in contact with flame previous?
A. No, sir.
Q. Then there must be a flame before there can be an explosion?
A. Yes, sir.

The only evidence as to the condition of things at that time coming from the knowledge of any eyewitness was the statement of the boy, Marvin Reynolds, made after the explosion to Dr. W.E. Craig, introduced in behalf of the defense, which will hereinafter be more fully considered.

The evidence of the plaintiff on the question of the priority of the fire was to the effect that in the basement underneath the apartment occupied by [Mr. and Mrs. Stevens] *there were several poles and books and barrels which were charred and burned…*[Fire Association of Philadelphia] *also offered evidence of the statements of the boy, Marvin Reynolds, made to Dr. Craig, which declarations were admitted in evidence…These statements were made soon after the explosion. The boy, when first discovered, was lying in the basement horribly mutilated, his skin burned off, his fingers charred—almost cooked—his knuckles loose and dropping off. He could not at first be seen by the witness because of the smoke and dust. His statements were, for the most part, incoherent, and he kept repeating his words and mumbling. He was taken upstairs, where he said to the witness, Dr. Craig: "How did this happen, or why did it happen? Don't let my folks know anything about it." He stated that he was down in the basement and struck a match. He kept saying one thing over and over again and mumbling—hardly intelligible—but at times he seemed to understand what he was saying, and then would go over the same statement again. Dr. Craig stated that the boy was found perhaps 15 to 20 feet from the foot of the stairs…we find the judgment of the trial court was for the right party.*

The judgment of the trial court is therefore affirmed.
COX, J., concurs. GRAY, J., not sitting.

It is unclear how many people passed away in the building during its long occupancy. However, when it closed, some of the remaining tenants who were forced to vacate the building had resided there for nearly half a century. The building has witnessed much emotion over the years, from celebrations and joy to horrific pain and death. Such locations can be the site of paranormal activity almost as if the emotion, whether positive or negative, imprints on the environment. This phenomenon can occur regardless of whether ghosts or apparitions are observed. Residual sounds can be heard, such as footsteps and voices, and abnormalities such as cold spots, floating light spheres, elevated electromagnetic field readings or unexplained spikes in EMF occur. There have been multiple accounts from people who have said that they or someone they knew experienced this type of activity over the years in the Olivia. Most of these reports often begin with "I had a friend who lived in the Olivia, and you would hear footsteps in their apartment and you would walk into the room where it was coming from and no one would be there" or "You would get the feeling you were being watched for no real reason." I have heard similar accounts from enough people that it is unlikely that these reports were borne out of pure imagination. For these reasons, when PSL had the opportunity to conduct a paranormal investigation at the Olivia, we readily took up the offer.

It was a cold winter evening when I first walked into the Olivia. I was accompanied by two other PSL team members and our guide. Even in the darkness, the beauty of the building was evident. We toured the building and had audio recorders with us. The heat was not on, and it was so cold that we could see our breath. As we toured the basement, it was difficult to keep our bearings at first in the pitch black darkness as our flashlight beams only illuminated a fraction of the huge spaces. The rooms were empty and stripped of décor. But our guide was able to tell us where the diner, billiards

The Olivia Apartment Building today. It is still a beautiful, imposing building. *Courtesy of the author.*

room and barbershop had been. As we approached the boiler room, we began discussing the explosion that had killed Marvin Reynolds and tried to figure out where Marvin would likely have been standing when he struck the match. As we walked around the area searching for evidence of the old natural gas lines (which would have run to a light fixture suspended from the ceiling), one of the audio recorders caught an EVP. The EVP was a deep male voice, saying, "I hate you Shag——." The last syllable was unintelligible. One of my team members present that evening has the nickname "Shaggy," but that fact had not been mentioned since we had arrived at the Olivia.

We proceeded through the building, moving floor by floor. As we moved down the hallway toward the apartment that reputedly belonged to Al Capone's aunt at one time, we passed a spot where wood beams formed an archway overhead. We reviewed the audio and found that an EVP had been

Paranormal Science sets up sound experiments in the lobby of the Olivia in order to test various frequencies for EVPs. *Courtesy of Paranormal Science Lab.*

caught. This time, the audio recorder caught an EVP of a woman's voice, which said, "Not through there with your gun." We each carried a flashlight, and two of us carried hand-held audio recorders. Whether this statement was directed at us, mistaking the devices as weapons, is unknown. Perhaps it was from a residual haunting, which replays a past event, oblivious to the present activity of living persons in the environment. Regardless of whether there was a connection to Al Capone or his men in that apartment, it was very common in the early days of the Olivia for men to carry weapons, and a number of gangsters and criminals spent time in the Joplin area, so it may refer to some past event now lost to history.

Our investigation spanned two nights and a day and involved almost three hundred hours of video, covering five floors and the basement, nearly one hundred hours of audio and hundreds of still photographs. The investigation produced several very interesting piece of evidence. In one apartment, a high-speed camera was set up on a tripod, and still photos were taken at the rate of thirty frames per second. The shutter speed was set at $1/1250$ of a second, and the frames were taken 0.03 seconds apart. Two consecutive frames captured a very bright light. The first shows the light anomaly on the right side of the photo near the doorway. The second shows the light anomaly on the left side of the photo. Calculating the distance between the two points where the light anomaly appears and the elapsed time means that the light anomaly was traveling at approximately three hundred miles per hour. The question was whether this light was caused by something natural, with the most common explanation being a flying insect, which can appear white when light from the camera flash reflects off its body. The most common culprit is a moth. However, the speed at which the light anomaly traversed the room was too fast to be an insect. The fastest flying insects are deer and horse flies, which have been clocked flying ninety miles per hour; the top speed for a moth is thirty-three miles per hour. As such, it seems unlikely that this light anomaly was the result of a bug flying through the frame. There was neither live electricity in the apartment nor any electronic or battery-operated device in the apartment at the time the photos were taken. There were no other investigators in the apartment besides the photographer at that time. The conclusion is that the light anomaly may have been paranormal in nature.

In another apartment, three investigators conducted an EVP session, asking questions and recording any responses or other sound anomalies. While the investigators asked questions in a bedroom, human footsteps were heard in the adjacent living room. No one was there, and no sign of an

Interior of an apartment at the Olivia. Notice the light anomaly on the right side of the frame. *Courtesy of Paranormal Science Lab.*

Interior of an apartment at the Olivia. Notice the light anomaly on the left side of the frame. The elapsed time between the previous frame and this one means it was traveling at approximately three hundred miles per hour. *Courtesy of Paranormal Science Lab.*

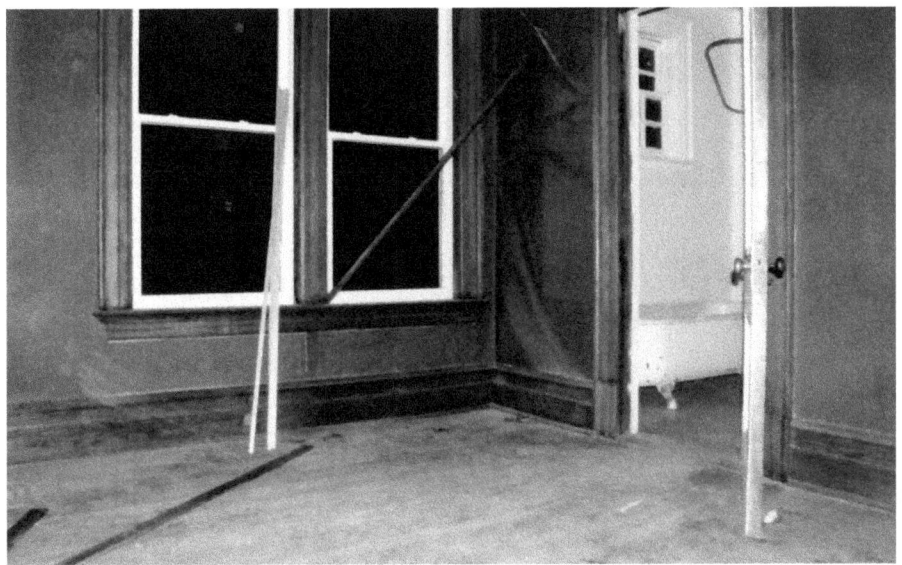

The orbs appearing in front of the window at the Olivia Apartment Building and on the left side of the photo are dust or pollen particles and not evidence of paranormal activity. *Courtesy of Paranormal Science Lab.*

animal was found. Investigators asked if any entity present would stand next to one of the investigators in the doorway, and the investigator reported feeling a cold draft, though none was detected.

In yet another apartment, where again there was no electricity, multiple groups of investigators encountered high, free-floating EMF readings in the air and away from the walls. Moreover, the area of high EMF was concentrated in the general shape and size of a person. Even more interesting was the fact that the area of high EMF would move about the room as if a person was walking around. It tended to "walk" around the investigators even as they repositioned themselves in another part of the room, and this happened repeatedly. Nothing was seen. Readings were taken to verify that there was not an elevated EMF reading from the wiring, and it was confirmed that there was no live electricity in the vicinity. This activity continued for about an hour. A natural EMF field does not move around, nor does an elevated reading from wiring or appliances. Precautions were taken by investigators to avoid inadvertently causing an EMF spike, such as turning off cell phones.

Several investigators had experiences in the formal dining room and kitchen on the fifth floor. Sounds were heard that reminded them of the sounds of a busy kitchen full of chefs preparing food, and the sounds of footsteps in the dining room were also heard. These may well be residual, imprinted on the apartment's environment and replaying like a recording. An extended EVP session in the lobby resulted in repeated responses, indicating that a young girl was present who had lived in the building with her mother. The responses seemed playful and childlike. However, there were responses that there was another entity in the building that the girl did not like. There was no indication whether this was related to the man's voice captured in the basement that said "I hate you Shag—." There was nothing unnerving in these responses. It appeared that whatever was present was indifferent to the living or, at most, was simply curious.

In the basement, the atmosphere was slightly different. On multiple occasions, investigators received responses in EVP sessions that indicated there were two separate male entities present. The first appeared to be Marvin Reynolds, the young man killed in the 1908 explosion. Responses indicated that Marvin felt the explosion was not his fault. The reason for this belief is mere speculation, but perhaps his spirit is unaware that the flame from the match ignited gas vapors, or perhaps there are facts that are unknown that led to the explosion, which Marvin was unable to communicate to Dr. Craig. The second presence seemed to be the deep voice in the EVP captured during our initial walkthrough. Responses from this entity centered on telling investigators to leave, but there was no clue as to the identity of this presence.

On subsequent investigations, PSL has documented additional activity at the Olivia, including the pump organ in the lobby playing notes on its own. The organ is not electric, and the foot pedals must be pumped in order to produce sound. In the same apartment that the free-floating EMF occurred, multiple investigators heard the voice of a woman saying "Visions." The voice and the investigators' reaction to it were captured on video and audio. Voices were heard in conversation along with the sounds of heavy furniture being dragged across the floor. On investigating the source, no one was found, and the dust on the floors where the sound came from was undisturbed.

The Olivia is an amazing building that is rich with history, and it played an important role in the development of Joplin. There may be paranormal activity inside its walls, but it is activity that I encourage people to experience should they have the opportunity. If the building is reopened in the future, it is doubtful many of the new occupants would notice strange happenings, except perhaps the occasional sound of footsteps or the feeling they heard someone speak when no one was there. Most likely, new occupants would assume they imagined the whole thing. However, should they notice these things, they will be in the company of those who have long held memories of the grand apartment building.

CHAPTER EIGHT
GANGSTERS AND THE SERIAL KILLER

Joplin continued to play host to outlaws of various kinds. The desperate times of the Great Depression spawned numerous bank robbers and criminals. Bank robberies during this time period were frequent occurrences in the Midwest, and far too many took place in Oklahoma and Missouri. Many of the gangsters, bank robbers and other fugitives found their way by traveling through Joplin during this time period. Herbert Allen "Deafy" Farmer grew up in Webb City, Missouri, and was a childhood acquaintance of Ma Barker and her sons. The Barker family lived in Webb City until 1915, when they moved to Tulsa, Oklahoma. The two families maintained their friendship through the years, and during the Great Depression, Herbert Farmer and his wife, Esther, ran a safe house in Joplin for gangsters to hide out in. The FBI summary on Ma Barker's "Karpis-Barker" gang concluded that the Barker boys had been taught their skills in crime by Herbert Farmer.

The Farmers were involved in the planning of the infamous Kansas City Massacre, during which four policemen were killed, along with Frank "Jelly" Nash. Prior to this, Nash had escaped from Leavenworth prison, had been captured and was being escorted through Union Station in Kansas City by federal agents who were returning him to Leavenworth. The Farmers were also involved in a plan that was formed at the Connor Hotel in Joplin to free Nash from the federal agents as they came through Joplin, but the plan was not carried out (although Mrs. Nash and gangsters from out of town had arrived and were staying with the Farmers). Instead, it was decided that it would be carried out at Union Station in Kansas City. This attempt to free Jelly Nash from federal custody resulted in the Kansas City Massacre.

Although the Barkers gave Farmer $2,500 to live on during the aftermath of the Kansas City Massacre, Farmer made statements to police during his interrogation, suggesting that the Barkers were involved in the Union Station shootings. The Barkers, however, were not involved: Pretty Boy Floyd was the trigger man. In 1934, Farmer was convicted of conspiracy to aid a federal prisoner escape and received the maximum sentence: two years in prison and a $10,000 fine. Esther Farmer was given probation and fined $5,000. Herbert Farmer served his sentence in Leavenworth and was then transferred to the new federal prison at Alcatraz. After his release, he returned to Joplin, where he and Esther lived until his death in 1948. Later, Esther married Harvey Bailey, known as the "dean of the American bank robbers." They remained in Joplin the rest of their lives. Bailey died in 1979, and Esther died in 1981.

Bonnie and Clyde: A Legend Is Born

Joplin's most well-known brush with Depression-era gangsters came in 1933, when Bonnie Parker and Clyde Barrow, along with other members of their gang, rented a garage apartment in south Joplin under assumed names. The Barrow gang had been in Joplin for about twelve days, and although they already were wanted in other states, they didn't bother to lie low, going out to dinner instead, seemingly unconcerned about being recognized. It is said that their favorite restaurant while in Joplin was Wilder's, which is still in business and in the same location on Main Street.

In a real sense, the legend of Bonnie and Clyde was born in Joplin, Missouri. The layover in Joplin is believed to have been set up by Clyde Barrow's brother, Buck, who had been pardoned by the governor of Texas and released from prison one week before the gang showed up in Joplin. Joplin was a good location for those on the run as it was just a few miles from both the Kansas and Oklahoma state lines. The Barrow gang could take advantage of the fact that law enforcement stopped at the state line in those days.

The garage apartment at 3347 Oak Ridge Drive actually faces Thirty-fourth Street. Suspicious neighbors, thinking that bootleggers had moved into the apartment, alerted the police on April 13, 1933. Five policemen responded with a search warrant just as Clyde Barrow and gang member W.D. Jones were arriving, and officers rushed to intercept them before they closed the garage door. In a shootout that lasted less than a minute, Clyde and Jones were injured and two officers were shot. Newton County constable John Wesley Harriman and Joplin detective Harry McGinnis were mortally wounded. The other gang members, including Bonnie Parker, ran down the stairs from the apartment and escaped in a stolen Ford V-8 sedan. They left in such haste that Bonnie and Buck Barrow's wife, Blanche, left their purses, in which the two women had placed stolen diamonds, tying the Barrow gang to a robbery of a milling business in Neosho, Missouri. Bullet damage can still be seen on the building's exterior, particularly on the lintel over the garage door. The fallen McGinnis was lying in the driveway, blocking the escape vehicle's path. Clyde waited while his brother pulled McGinnis out of the way before taking off at a high rate of speed.

What they left behind in this garage apartment contributed to the legend of Bonnie and Clyde as folk heroes for a nation that was weary of the harsh conditions of the Great Depression and a bit envious of the

The Bonnie and Clyde garage apartment hideout at 3347 Oak Ridge Drive in south Joplin. It appears today very much as it did on that fateful day in April 1933, when two policemen were fatally gunned down on this driveway. *Courtesy of the author.*

Reproduction of the wanted poster for Bonnie and Clyde issued by the Joplin Police Department. *Courtesy of the author.*

criminals who were seen as fighting the system that was victimizing the nation's people. Bonnie and Clyde were also made human by what they left behind in haste. Bonnie wrote poetry, and one of her poems was left behind. Also, undeveloped film was found. The film contained candid pictures of

Bonnie and Clyde and included the iconic images by which they are now remembered. It was developed, and the pictures were printed in the *Joplin Globe*, which also printed Bonnie's poem. The photos included a candid pose of Bonnie smoking a cigar and Clyde holding her up in the air. Another photo shows Bonnie poking a sawed-off shotgun at Clyde's chest, and these images gave her the reputation as a gun moll, although it is now accepted that she never shot a gun.

The Joplin apartment hideout has been a place of macabre interest for decades, and many have driven by to get a glimpse of the building. I have heard speculation of paranormal activity around the garage. People speak of a foreboding feeling. While the outlaws were living life almost with a death wish, which can produce intense emotion, it is not clear that Bonnie and Clyde are responsible for the uneasy feeling some experience. It would seem more likely that the dying McGinnis and Harriman are responsible. Although the shootout at the apartment was tragic, the film that was found there contributed to the legend that Bonnie and Clyde have become in the ensuing decades. Those unforgettable images also contributed to their deaths, for it was with those photos that law enforcement tracked them down and ultimately killed them in a grisly ambush in Louisiana a year after Bonnie and Clyde left Joplin.

Billy Cook: Murderous Hitchhiker

The oldest cemetery in western Jasper County is Peace Church Cemetery, which is one-quarter of a mile from the Rader Farm. It appears abandoned to the casual guest. While it has suffered vandalism over the years, it isn't abandoned. At times, it appears surreal due to ugly scorch marks and scars to the ground, trees and tombstones from controlled burns used to manage the thick prairie grasses that continuously threaten to reclaim the land. The first burial in Peace Church Cemetery predates the founding of the cemetery and even the church for which it is named. Back in the days when there were only a handful of settlers in the area, there was a trail that was used by salt haulers to travel from Springfield, Missouri, all the way to the western portion of Indian Territory (present-day Oklahoma) to the salt flats where they would get salt. During one such trip, a slave of a salt hauler passed away from illness while the expedition was camped nearby. This spot was chosen for his burial because the men decided it had a nice view. The

The sign on the gate to Peace Church Cemetery. As you walk through the cemetery, you sense the long span of time represented by the tombstones. *Courtesy of the author.*

cemetery has been in continuous use since the 1850s. The church has been gone for many years.

There have been claims of ghosts and paranormal activity at Peace Church Cemetery for years. Most of this activity has been connected to the infamous killer William Edward "Billy" Cook, who is buried in the cemetery. Cook grew up in Joplin, having been abandoned along with his siblings by a drunkard father after their mother died. Billy did not fare well at the hands of his foster mother, a woman who was cruel to him, in part because he had a birth defect that left Billy unable to close one eyelid. It wasn't long before Cook was in trouble with the law and ended up in court for truancy at the age of twelve. Billy asked to be sent to reformatory school rather than be sent back to his foster mother. At age seventeen, he was transferred to the Missouri State Penitentiary. While at the penitentiary in Jefferson City, Cook attacked another inmate with a baseball bat. He was released from prison at age twenty-one, and he returned to Joplin. He attempted to reunite with his father, who still lived in Joplin, but it apparently did not go well, and soon Billy told his father he intended "to live by the gun and roam." This was in 1950, and Billy hitchhiked his way to California, ending up in the small desert town of Blythe, where he worked in a diner as a dishwasher, the only job he ever held. While there, he worked with a woman named Cecilia who treated him with kindness.

In late December 1950, he drifted east to Texas and picked up a .32-caliber revolver. It was at this point that Cook began his twenty-two-day crime spree. On December 30, 1950, mechanic Lee Archer was driving near Lubbock, Texas, when he picked up Billy Cook, who was hitchhiking. Cook robbed Archer of $100 at gunpoint and forced him into the trunk of his car. Archer was able to escape by forcing open the trunk with a tire iron and jumping out as Cook made a slow turn onto a secondary road. After the car ran out of fuel on the highway between Claremore and Tulsa, Oklahoma, Cook posed again as a hitchhiker.

Soon the extent of Cook's mental instability became apparent. He got a ride with the Mosser family, who were en route to New Mexico on vacation. It was common to hitchhike and to pick up hitchhikers at that time, and Carl Mosser probably didn't think twice about helping out the young man who pretended to have car trouble with the car stolen from Archer. Cook forced Mosser to drive around aimlessly for three days. At one point, Mosser nearly wrestled the gun from Cook at a filling station near Wichita Falls, Texas, but Cook overpowered him. Finally, Mrs. Mosser and the children started crying hysterically, and Cook killed them all, even the family dog. He drove the blood-soaked car to Joplin and dumped the bodies in an abandoned mine shaft outside the city. The car was later found in Oklahoma just as it had been after the shootings, blood soaked with the seats riddled with bullet holes. But Cook made a fatal mistake and left the receipt for the revolver he had purchased in Texas in the Mosser car, giving authorities a name for their suspect.

Cook returned to Blythe, California. Deputy Sheriff Homer Waldrip became suspicious that the Billy Cook his wife Cecilia had worked with at the restaurant there was the man described in the wanted bulletins that had been sent out by Oklahoma law enforcement. Waldrip went to the motel Billy had lived at when working at the diner to question the man who had shared the room with Cook, but he was surprised when he was met at the motel room door by Cook himself. Waldrip was taken hostage and held at gunpoint with his own gun. As with Carl Mosser, Waldrip was made to drive around without a clear destination. After driving for about forty miles, Cook ordered the deputy to pull over. He made Waldrip lie facedown in a ditch and told him he was going to shoot him in the back of the head. While Waldrip awaited the gunshot, Cook walked back to the deputy's patrol car, got in and drove away. Cook later told reporters why he didn't shoot Waldrip; it was because the deputy's wife, Cecilia, had always been so nice to him, had treated him like a human being and had been nicer than anyone had ever been to him all his life.

Next, Cook kidnapped another motorist, Robert Dewey, from Seattle. At some point while driving in the California desert, the traveling salesman tried to wrestle the gun from Cook but was wounded in the process. While they struggled, the car swerved off the road. Cook murdered Dewey with a shot to the head and left his body in a ditch. Cook then kidnapped two men, James Burke and Forrest Damron, who were on a hunting trip. He forced them to drive across the Mexican border, and they ended up in the Mexican town of Santa Rosalia. By this point, law enforcement throughout the Southwest was looking for Cook.

He couldn't outrun the bulletins circulating about him. Cook was recognized by Santa Rosalia police chief Luis Parra, who walked up to Cook and grabbed the .32 revolver from his belt before Cook could react. Cook was placed under arrest and returned to the border, where FBI agents were waiting to take him into custody. "I hate everybody's guts," Cook said at the time of his arrest, "and everybody hates mine."

Cook was returned to Oklahoma to stand trial for the murders of the Mosser family. He underwent psychological testing, and seven psychiatrists gave their opinions as to Cook's competency to stand trial. Three concluded he was competent while the other four concluded that he was not. What all seven could agree on was that Billy Cook was a psychopath. The judge made his own compromise, ruling that Cook was competent enough to stand trial but should not be put to death. Cook was convicted of murdering the five members of the Mosser family and sentenced to three hundred years in prison. Cook was then allowed to be extradited to California to stand trial for the murder of the Seattle salesman, Robert Dewey. He was convicted and sentenced to death. Cook was remanded to death row at San Quentin prison.

During his time at San Quentin, Cook crossed paths with Edward Bunker, who later became an actor and successful author and screenwriter. Bunker shared a similar childhood with Cook and was in and out of prison until 1975, when he was released and turned to writing and acting. In his memoir, *Education of a Felon*, Bunker describes attacking Cook while in the showers with a shank, cutting him several times before being hauled away into solitary confinement by guards.

On December 12, 1952, Cook was executed in the gas chamber at San Quentin Prison. Billy Cook was to be used by one more person after his death. Glen Boydstun was a mortician in Comanche, Oklahoma, who had been around long enough to remember crowds paying to see bullet-riddled bodies of old west outlaws, and more recently in 1934, the body of Pretty Boy Floyd had attracted more than forty thousand people to pay to see it in Sallisaw, Oklahoma. The bodies of Ma Barker and Fred Barker met a similar fate after they were killed in 1935.

Boydstun decided to try his luck at the death display of Billy Cook in Comanche, despite the fact that the town had absolutely nothing to do with Cook or his crimes. Boydstun contacted Will Cook in Joplin and said he would be willing to foot the bill for a proper burial for his wayward son. Will Cook signed his permission for Boydstun to claim the body at San Quentin, and the mortician pointed his hearse toward California. Three days after the execution, Cook's corpse—outfitted in a suit and tie—was on public display in Comanche. Boydstun was dissatisfied with the initial day's box-office proceeds, so he added loudspeakers and acted like a sideshow barker, calling spectators to see "the last American desperado." Thousands came on the second day, including busloads of schoolchildren. In all, as many as twelve thousand people saw the body before Cook's siblings intervened. They hired a lawyer, wrestled their brother's corpse away from Boydstun and returned it to Joplin.

One of Billy's sisters paid to have his body returned to Joplin. Under the cover of darkness (in order to avoid the press), Cook's body was interred in the family plot at Peace Church Cemetery. As this news spread, there was a public outcry and opposition to the burial of the infamous killer in the cemetery. Billy Cook's grave was quietly moved just outside the original grounds of the cemetery but still near the family plot.

Cook has become a focus of local occult interest over the years. It is common to go to the cemetery and find piles of items left in various spots that people believe is where Cook's unmarked grave lies: flowers, pieces of folded paper, candles and various keepsakes. It has been rumored that teenagers have, at times, congregated in attempts to contact the soul of Billy Cook. In 1987, three seventeen-year-old boys from nearby Carl Junction, Missouri, had been engaging in animal sacrifices and ended up committing what is termed a "thrill-killing" of a nineteen-year-old acquaintance of theirs, beating him to death with a baseball bat because they simply wanted the thrill of a kill. During the murder trial, they claimed they were involved in satanic worship and were somehow influenced by the spirit of Billy Cook to commit murder at the time. The boys were convicted of murder.

Billy Cook was the inspiration of the film noir classic *The Hitchhiker*, the plot of which involves a man kidnapping two men and forcing them to drive to Mexico. In the movie, two men on a fishing trip pick up a hitchhiker named Emmett Myers, who turns out to be a psychopathic serial killer. *The Hitchhiker* went into production on June 24, 1952. It was Ida Lupino's first

Peace Church Cemetery, overlooking the area where Billy Cook lies in an unmarked grave. *Courtesy of the author.*

fast-paced film after having directed four films about social issues. Lupino interviewed the two men whom Billy Cook had held hostage and got releases from them and also from Cook's father, so that she could integrate parts of Cook's life into the script. To appease the censors, she reduced the number of deaths to three. *The Hitchhiker* premiered on March 20, 1953, and had the tagline "When was the last time you invited death into your car?"

There is another legend that Billy Cook was the inspiration for the classic rock song "Riders on the Storm" by The Doors. According to band member Robby Krieger, the song was modeled after "(Ghost) Riders in the Sky" and even contains sound effects such as rain and thunder. But the darker theory is that the song's lyrics describe the exploits of Billy Cook. "Riders on the Storm" was the last song recorded by The Doors before Jim Morrison died in July 1971. Whether or not there is any truth to the theory probably will never be known. Supporters of the theory point to the following verse:

> *There's a killer on the road*
> *His brain is squirming like a toad*
> *Take a long holiday*
> *Let your children play*
> *If you give this man a ride, sweet memory will die*
> *Killer on the road*

Haunted Joplin

In his book *L.A. Despair: A Landscape of Crimes and Bad Times*, author John Gilmore details firsthand accounts of encounters with Billy Cook from Los Angeles on to Blythe shortly before the killing spree began. Below is one man's account:

The only light leaking into the alley was the sheen from a Jesus Saves *sign blinking orange and red across the dirty asphalt. Seventy-six-year-old Gerald Stewart remembers that night. "So black," he says, "you could hardly see your hand at your face. Bums that couldn't get into the mission slept against the back of a building behind Main. You had to be careful where you pissed."*

Stewart says he'd been in the alley dozens of times, but that night God had to be looking the other way. "I got the hell scared right out of me by the kid coming at me in the dark, right on top of me and twisting his hands around that length of pipe like rolling a paper to beat a dog. First thought I had was he's got a gun, figurin' I was seein' a barrel. It was 1950 and I remember it like yesterday. A couple days after Thanksgiving, it was.

"Soon as I could see his face, I recognized him. I had a janitor job at the Midnight Mission, and the kid'd slept in the flop a cot or two down from mine. He'd watched me stick some bills in the sock of one foot, and he kept watchin', even layin' there with that one eye open in the dark. Gave me the damn heebie-jeebies, that street lamp shining in and near lightin' that eye he didn't close.

"It wasn't a gun the kid had, only a hunk of pipe, [and he was] squeezin' it, like gettin' ready to bust my head," says Stewart. "He had tattooed words on the fingers of his hand, and I didn't know which was worse to die by—bein' shot or gettin' my brains knocked in. He had a look the same as a dead man you got propped on its feet, and he was sayin', 'I want you to know I ain't eat nothin' since day before yesterday...I've been on this sidewalk and I hate this stinkin' city more'n I hate anything.' 'What do you hate about it?' I asked. 'You got free turkey and gravy two nights ago, didn't you?' I said, trying not to show he worried me. He kept lookin' me in the eye and he said, 'I just told you I hate this stinkin' city...' Sayin' all that like he's telling the time of day, and I said, 'Well, fella, I do feel for you. I ain't found no city that ain't stinking to me neither.' He didn't say nothin', in fact I figured I could say anything and he wouldn't've heard any of it, just a starin' with that eye holdin' still like a damned cat fixin' on a rat. But I didn't feel like any rat with what I'd been through in the War—enough to make you puke the whole thing. Italy and damned Germany and I was thinkin' it's a helluva way to go, a squint-eyed kid who looked like a fire plug about to bust my head with a shit-house pipe."

Stewart dug in his pockets. "I tried savin' my hide and gave him what scratch I came up with. Maybe it was eleven bucks. Could've been less since I'd bought and drunk a pint before goin' in the alley to piss, and then him spottin' me where I'd gone, like he was a black shape comin' out of the shadows. I'd also bought smokes and just about was doin' my business when he was standin' there, same kid that'd wolfed the grub at the mission."

After staring at the older man for several moments, the kid said, "I seen you coming in here down that end, and I said here's a regular guy that'll help me out 'cause I gotta get to Barstow."

Stewart said, "What the hell's in Barstow?"

"This turn-around collar guy," the kid said, "gave me a card of a guy he knows there. Told me I can get fixed up with work in Barstow."

"Work?" Stewart said. "In Barstow? That's the middle of the damned desert." Stewart handed him the crumpled bills. "He looked at it in my hand and kept looking like he was still contemplatin' the use of that pipe on me even though I was giving him the scratch. I said I was glad I ran into him before I spent it 'cause I always tried helpin' a fella. He said that was white of me and he let go of the pipe—gave a toss and it clanked on the alley and rattled as he walked away. Didn't say nothin' else. 'Course later when I learnt from the newspaper who he was and

Broken tombstones and torch marks catch the eye as you look across Peace Church Cemetery. Somewhere out there are unmarked graves of Civil War soldiers. Perhaps they are doomed to linger here. *Courtesy of the author.*

all that stuff about him bein' the most dangerous man in the country, I knew I'd walked off with my life instead of layin' with my brains in the alley.

"After givin' him the bucks, I didn't go to the flop for fear he hadn't taken off for Barstow or wherever the hell he was goin'. I got my gear and nosed over to the Salvation Army to hear some singing about the Lord. I figured I owed the Son of God my life and I'd say a prayer of thanks for Him lettin' me live by sendin' that miserable boy on his miserable way."

So does Billy Cook linger in Peace Church Cemetery? People experience fear, anxiety and a sinking feeling as they walk in the cemetery, particularly at night. Shadow people are seen as a routine matter, often leaning out from behind the scattered trees and tombstones, watching the living. I have observed shadow people in the cemetery. However, they are most commonly seen in an area on the opposite side of the cemetery from Cook's unmarked grave. "Graveyard lights" (or ghost lights) have also been observed, appearing as balls of light floating in the air amid tombstones. Few people feel comfortable standing in the cemetery after dark. However, Billy Cook may not be the only source of these feelings. What few people know is that there are a number of unmarked graves of Civil War soldiers who had been killed in the area buried in Peace Church Cemetery. Most of these sit on the opposite side from Billy Cook, in the area where shadow people are often seen. Perhaps the soldiers and Billy Cook are in an eternal standoff, all locked in their own personal battles with demons of the past.

CHAPTER NINE
PARANORMAL MYSTERIES AND LEGENDS

There are a number of unexplained phenomena in the Joplin area that may or may not be actual hauntings but certainly are paranormal in nature. They are no less intriguing than the ghost stories that abound. The element of the unknown has caused much speculation and attempted explanation over the years. However, none of the following tales has been satisfactorily explained.

THE HORNET SPOOKLIGHT

The Hornet Spooklight is the most infamous site of paranormal activity in southwest Missouri. It has also been called the Joplin Spooklight and the Tri-State Spooklight, but local residents associate it a small town called Hornet, which once stood nearby. Just south of Joplin, in the area where Hornet once stood, is what is commonly referred to as Spooklight Road, a county road in Newton County that runs into Oklahoma to the west. Many have incorrectly called the road the Devil's Promenade. This is incorrect, as the Devil's Promenade is a natural feature, a portion of the bluff overlooking Spring River located two miles west of where the Spooklight is observed. Legends of the Spooklight have appeared in print since shortly after the

Civil War. However, the sightings are even older. The first known reports of the mysterious lights came in 1836, during the forced march of Native Americans to Indian Territory (Oklahoma), better known as the Trail of Tears. It appears to be an earthlight, similar to those seen in other parts of the world. It will appear as a ball of luminescent, free-floating light that bounces a few feet above the roadway, in the trees along the road and in adjacent fields. It has been observed for over 170 years.

There are several legends about the Spooklight, but two are heard most frequently. One suggests that the light is that of two young Indian lovers searching for each other after they killed themselves when their chief refused to grant permission for them to marry. The other claims it belongs to a Civil War soldier who was killed in battle and is now searching for his unit.

The legend of the Indian lovers has been handed down by the Quapaw tribe that lives in this vicinity. According to legend, a handsome young Indian brave fell in love with a beautiful Indian maiden of the Quapaw tribe. The young Indians were desperately in love, and it seems that the old chief, the father of the maiden, tried to take undue advantage of the situation by asking for an unusually large payment for his daughter's hand. Being unable to meet the demands of the Indian chief, the couple decided to elope. They had scarcely reached the outside of the camp area when their absence was discovered. The chief became very angry and sent out a large group of warriors to pursue the young brave and his daughter. The young maiden knew that she would be severely punished and that her lover would be killed. Knowing that they were going to be captured, the young couple decided to commit suicide by leaping from a high rocky cliff overlooking Spring River. This spot is now known as "Lovers' Leap" or "Devil's Promenade." It is believed that the spirits of the young Indian couple return nightly to form the phenomenon seen today.

A large Indian powwow and stomp dance are held annually in the Spooklight area, and it is attended by thousands from near and far. The bridge crossing Spring River near the Devil's Promenade is called Devil's Promenade Bridge.

One of the less well-known legends about the Spooklight comes from the Osage Indians, who occupied this area before the Quapaw Indians. According to this legend, the light is the spirit of the Osage Indian chief who had been beheaded on the Devil's Promenade, and the light was said to be his torch as he searches for his missing head.

Other legends arose out of the early mining in the area, including this tale told by Roy Grainger and documented in *The Tri-State Spooklight* by Bob Loftin.

This section of the Ozarks has its own superstitions and folklore. Here, too, the Indians have "handed down" many tales from generation to generation. I thought of all this the first time I heard the light being discussed…Finally one night a bunch of us met to [go] see the light. One of the fellows had been there many times and as we drove along he told the story about the time when lead and zinc were discovered in the area back in the 1870's [sic]. Many miners lived in the area. One of the miners lived here off the Spook Light road, just a "stone's throw" from the Indian Territory. One night his cabin was raided by the Indians while he was away working in the mines. His children were kidnapped and he never saw them again. It is said he took his lantern and started to look for them. He was never seen again. The light down the road as seen now is believed by many to be the miner returning night after night with his lantern still in search of his lost children.

This story prompted another fellow in the car to say that he had been told that a number of years ago a small child from a miner's family had wandered off into the woods and was never seen again by her family. She has become somewhat of a "nature girl" with witchlike features who travels at night with a lantern in quest of food. This girl—the teller says—has actually been seen.…We turned onto the road to watch the light…and there it was!! My first impression was of an invisible person walking down the road with a lantern in his hand. As he walked the lantern would swing to and fro. Then it seemed to disappear as if going off into the woods only to reappear at another point…

View from a crossroad off Spooklight Road. The light is seen throughout this area as well, and shadow people have been observed in the fields and pastures along the road. *Courtesy of the author.*

Another time a group of boys and myself took a rifle to see if we could shoot the light... On this particular night there was a slight sprinkling of rain, but no fog. We stopped our car when we judged the distance between the light and ourselves to be approximately a half-block, we started to shoot. As we shot, the light seemed to dance from side to side as though dodging the bullets. Needless to say we never did hit our target.

Residents living along Spooklight Road have long told of their own experiences over the years. Some almost give a personality to the mysterious light. Here is one such account that also appears in Loftin's book:

Having lived on State Line road near the area where the "Ghost Light" is located, I have seen it hundreds of times. I can remember about 1942 when a group of students from Michigan University came down and camped out for 2 weeks in the vicinity of the "Spook Light." They performed every test they could, even shooting at it with high powered rifles, but they found out nothing. An old timer, the late Charley Dawes, who lived three-fourths of a mile off the road for 70 years, told me his father had seen the "Ghost Light" even before his son was born. A number of times we have left people in a parked car and walked down the road a mile or so, only to have the light appear between us and the car.

And here is another from Chester McMinn:

My folks used to call the light "jack-o-lantern" when we moved here some 30 years ago. The old "lantern" and I got along pretty good together until about 2½ years ago. Seems the old light felt real neighborly one night and decided to help me with my plowing. It gets hot here during the day so I do a lot of plowing late in the evening. I couldn't see too well and I guess the old light sensed it, because he started hovering all over the field where I was plowing. He made a dart in my direction and I [was] absolutely "froze[n] stiff" to the tractor. I was too frightened to run. He must have seen my pre-dicament because just about then he sailed out of sight.

This final account comes from Mrs. John Bryan and is also from Loftin's book:

We moved to this section in 1918, and have seen the light often, especially around the first part of July each year. This is just about the time the Indians are having their stomp-dances down at the bridge. The Old Indian Medical Spring is on our property. Indians have come from all over, including the well-known Frank Vallier,

Vintage photograph of the Spooklight. The light is shown at the crest of the far hill in the road. *Courtesy of the author.*

to drink from this spring. A number of Indians are buried here in the hillside above the spring. It is in this gully where the spring lies that the old light bounces around like a big ball. Why it always appears here the first part of July, I don't know. All the while it's here it bounces up and down this gully as far as you can see.

Research has been conducted to explain the light, but results have been less than explanatory. One theory is that the light is actually the light from cars' headlights from I-44 several miles away. However, the light was observed decades before the road was there and before cars were invented. Another theory is that the light is a natural phenomenon: swamp gas, caused by luminous gases rising from decaying organic matter. But the land is not swampy, and such gases have not been found in the area.

I have witnessed the Hornet Spooklight on multiple occasions over twenty-odd years. I have no idea what the light is, but it appears to have unique properties. It can split into multiple balls, and on one occasion when I was with several people, we divided ourselves into two groups, stood a couple of hundred yards apart and faced each other. The light appeared between the two groups. Everyone in my group could see the light, which was about

A view of how Spooklight Road appeared during the daytime prior to the road being paved gives no hint of the amazing sights awaiting a visitor at night. Paving the road has resulted in more activity on the next section of road. *Courtesy of the author.*

seventy-five yards in front us. The other group, at seeing our reaction to the light, started walking toward us. As they neared, someone in our group called out asking if they saw the light. "Where?" was the reply, and they kept walking until they were within a few feet of the light, which then abruptly disappeared. Joining us, the other group confirmed that they never saw the light; it was viewed from one direction only.

THE DEVIL'S PROMENADE

The Devil's Promenade has its own supernatural tale. Although it has long been associated with the local Indians in the area, the legend is of the Devil. Since the 1800s, stories have been told that the Devil will appear at the bluff overlooking Spring River, not far from where the Spooklight is seen.

For years, there was a wooden bridge that spanned Spring River at this point. It has been replaced with a modern concrete bridge. According to

Left: Vintage photograph of a wooden bridge in the Joplin area that is very similar to the original Devil's Promenade Bridge. *Courtesy of the author.*

Below: The new Devil's Promenade Bridge. Hoofbeats are no longer heard, and it doesn't shake like the old bridge, but it is said that the unwary can still summon the Devil here. *Courtesy of the author.*

Vintage postcard of the Devil's Promenade mailed in August 1905. Note reads, "Devil's Promenade, Dear Clyde. This is a sample of Kansas territory only it is not in Kansas. 4 Miles south. Come and see it. Indians in foreground." *Courtesy of the author.*

the legend, if you crossed the bridge at midnight (or, in some versions, stood in the middle of the bridge over the water), you would hear hoofbeats, and the floor of the bridge would shake as if horses were thundering across it. It was believed you were hearing the Devil cross the bridge. Additionally, it was said that if you crossed the bridge and returned ten times (or three times, by some accounts) at midnight, the Devil would appear. As previously discussed, the Devil's Promenade is connected to explanations for the Spooklight, often involving a death occurring on the bluff. It's worth noting also that Devil's Promenade does have a history of being used by the Indians for ceremonial purposes.

Some of the local Indian tribes have another legend as well. According to this legend, the "Little People" visit the Devil's Promenade, and if

The Devil's Promenade overlooking Spring River. What secrets does it hold? *Courtesy of the author.*

sweets are put out for them on the bridge, the Little People will come and take them and perhaps present themselves to you. This can happen during the day as well as at night. Little People are supposed to be small creatures that are only a couple of feet tall and look like Indians, and their hair is said to fall down to the ground. They are spiritual beings and are known to be tricksters. It is believed that seeing a Little Person is bad luck, and should you see them, you should not speak of it. In many accounts, they are described as being similar to fairies in Irish folklore, which are not friendly and can be very dangerous.

HOFFMAN MANSION

Another site within a mile of Spooklight Road and the Devil's Promenade is the Hoffman Mansion property. The land belonged to the Quapaw-Hoffman family. The patriarch made a fortune in the early oil fields of Oklahoma and then built a fine home for his large family. The family suffered through smallpox epidemics, and the lives of several of the children were claimed by the disease. Over time, descendants allowed the property to sit empty. The mansion burned to the ground, and all that remains are remnants of the foundation. At one point, it was rented out to a couple who ran a summer camp for children for several years. The camp became unprofitable, and it closed. Partial remains of the caretaker's house still stand. The family cemetery sits within sight of the road. At some point, a fence was erected to discourage people from trampling through the property.

Stories of murder and ghosts grew over the years. There was an urban legend that the people who ran the summer camp murdered children and buried them on the property. There is no evidence that this ever

From the road, you can see what remains of the caretaker's house on the grounds of Hoffman Mansion. *Courtesy of the author.*

The site is still referred to as the Hoffman Mansion, but the house burned down long ago and this is what remains. *Courtesy of the author.*

happened, and the story is likely born out of misunderstanding the children's graves that sit on the property, attributing them to murder rather than the smallpox epidemic of the late 1800s. Ghost lights have been seen at night, floating on the air across the ruins of buildings. It is also said that shadow people can be seen running across the prairie grass at night and the sound of them running, crunching grass and twigs underfoot, can also be heard. I have heard quite a few people recount stories of encountering the unexplained at the Hoffman Mansion and leaving the mansion very frightened.

Ew-wah and the Goatman

Another Indian tribe in the area is the Seneca Cayuga. Originally, they comprised two of the five tribes that formed the Iroquois League. Portions of the tribe are settled in various places from New York to Oklahoma to Canada. They, like the Quapaw Indians, have ceremonial land within two or three miles of the Devil's Promenade and the Spooklight. The land is said to be inhabited by the spirits of their ancestors, who reportedly appear as full-bodied apparitions at times, often along a ridge. They are said to stand silent, watching out over the land and the houses where some of the tribal members still live. The Seneca Indians have their own legend of shadow people, which they refer to as Ew-wah (this is the phonetic spelling). It is believed that the Ew-wah are more than shadows; they are physical in the sense that if you walk into them, it is as if you have walked into a person. These shadow people are not believed to be the benevolent spirits of ancestors like the apparitions seen in this area but are instead believed to be bad spirits that should be avoided. This is similar to theories in the field of paranormal investigations in that some believe there are two kinds of shadow persons: those believed to be human spirits and those believed not to be human spirits. Traditional practices to cleanse homes are used as precautions, such as placing cedar twigs and sage over windows and doorways.

There is also a creature referred to as the Goatman. It has been seen by tribal members for many years and is described as a large bipedal creature covered in long, dark fur. Its fur covers the entire face so that no features are visible; all you see is fur. This description mirrors those given of Bigfoot. Their similarities in appearance diverge at this point, for there are two large protrusions on either side of the Goatman's head that look like bone, similar to a goat's horns. The Goatman is said to live in the wooded hills and caves dotting this land. While receiving a tour of the land, several members of PSL were shown the area known as Goatman's Hollow, where the creature has been seen while men were out hunting. Several of us noticed the distinct sound of footsteps along the ridge above us as we walked about two miles down a valley. However, no creature was spotted. Our guide informed us that a few years earlier, conservation agents came in to help clear the stream bed to preventing flooding and ran across the Goatman. The agents told the landowners of the incident and said that they were threatened by the Goatman and shot a rifle at it. They believed it was wounded and that it scrambled up a hillside away from the men. As the agents left, they commented that they would not come back without a shotgun.

HAUNTED JOPLIN

THE JOPLIN F5 TORNADO: NEW PARANORMAL QUESTIONS

On May 22, 2011, disaster struck Joplin in the form of an F5 tornado with reported winds of up to 399 miles per hour. The tornado cut a straight path through the southern half of Joplin, a path that was almost a mile wide and thirteen miles long. Over nine thousand structures were affected, and thousands of homes were completely destroyed. One hundred sixty people

Top: Aftermath and destruction of the F5 tornado that devastated nine thousand structures in Joplin on May 22, 2011. *Courtesy of Alex Martin.*

Bottom: The tornado claimed 160 lives. The amount of destruction was difficult to comprehend in the days following the storm. *Courtesy of Alex Martin.*

Mural in commemoration of the tragic May 22, 2011 F5 tornado that devastated one-third of Joplin, Missouri. Children's accounts of butterfly people coming to the assistance of victims is incorporated in the painted images. Hints of paranormal intervention are included in the colorful tribute to the people who rode out the tornado that claimed 160 lives. *Courtesy of the author.*

lost their lives, making this tornado one of the deadliest in U.S. history. The massive funnel was not anticipated as it was hidden behind a rain wall on radar, and the cell did not follow the predicted path. The brunt of the tornado struck St. John's Regional Health Center and moved the massive nine-story hospital off of its foundation by five inches.

As injured people started pouring into the emergency rooms of other area hospitals and were rescued by first responders, a tale was repeated numerous times within those first hours. This tale came from the youngest victims. Over and over, throughout the affected zone, young children described how they were saved as the tornado raged around them. They described beings of white light coming and holding them and others down while the winds fought to suck them up off the ground. It would be understandable if the children said they saw angels, but they didn't. Consistently, they referred to these beings as "the butterfly people," describing them as having wings like butterflies and not the feathered, birdlike wings associated with angels. These accounts were given independently by many children who had no contact with each other, making it seem more credible that they were describing

something seen by a large number of children over a fairly large area. The tales were so pervasive that the butterfly people were referenced in a mural that was painted on the side of a building on Main Street. Whether the butterfly people were angels, ghosts or another type of entity is unknown.

CHAPTER TEN
The Connor Hotel

OPULENCE AND TRAGEDY

Walking up toward Joplin Public Library, one would not assume it to be the site of paranormal activity and would definitely not associate it with the history of the ground on which it sits. Like most of downtown Joplin, it is not the first building to sit on this spot. It's the third building to sit on the south end of the west side of Main Street between Third and Fourth Streets. Many are familiar with the Connor Hotel, which once stood on this spot before the library was built. Many more would be surprised to know that the Connor Hotel was not the first building on this location. J.H. McCoy was the first to build a hotel on the northwest corner of Fourth and Main Streets. The Joplin Hotel was a three-story brick building and the largest and most impressive hotel in the young city when it opened in April 1875. No tale of any haunting or deaths is known from this time period, but both are certainly possible.

Thomas O'Connor was an Irish immigrant and one of Joplin's first millionaires. He shortened his last name to Connor at some point after arriving in the United States, and he and his family settled in Tiffin, Ohio. Connor attempted to show his patriotism for his new country by trying to enlist as a twelve-year-old in the Civil War, but he was not accepted. Instead, he settled for a position as newsboy. This was just the beginning of a series of endeavors Thomas Connor undertook that eventually led him to Joplin and made him a fortune in the mining industry. He ended up in the cattle drives that originated in Texas, and while driving a herd of steers northward, he settled in Seneca, Missouri.

Above: The Joplin Public Library, which now sits where the Connor Hotel stood from 1907 to 1978. *Courtesy of the author.*

Left: Vintage postcard mailed April 5, 1912, from Will Beam to Ms. Violet Archer. Beam is asking Ms. Archer to come see him where he is working on a pump with two other men at Seventh and Joplin Streets on Saturday evening at 7:30 p.m. He ended the note with "I trust you will be thare." *Courtesy of the author.*

The Connor Hotel was a picture of luxury that pampered its guests and made a loud statement about the success of Joplin. *Courtesy of the Joplin Public Library.*

When he found his way to the young mining town, he bought tracts of land that produced significant lead and zinc yields, including in the Prosperity area. He took advantage of other business opportunities, partnering with a man named W. Kilgore, establishing two hack lines and making daily trips to Carthage and Neosho. Connor also went into the hotel business by purchasing, along with partners Tom Jones and E.Z. Wallower, the Joplin Hotel Company.

The Joplin Hotel became the setting for an elaborate April Fool's joke that proved Tom Connor was quite the practical joker. Detailed planning was required to carry out the prank. The joke began with the arrest of an elderly female employee of the Joplin Hotel Company who worked as a maid. When eleven silver spoons disappeared one day, she was promptly arrested. Apparently, the case seemed to be a strong one against the woman. Frank Lee, whom she retained as counsel, requested that Tom Connor have the charges dismissed. Connor agreed and informed the hotel's manager, Mr. Moats, who had filed the police report. Connor then took the opportunity to play a joke on Tom Jones. He hired attorney Richard Graham to draw up the petition for a fake $20,000 damage suit that was "filed" by the elderly maid for false imprisonment. The sheriff's office was the next piece of the puzzle for a convincing practical joke. Deputy Clarence Rier found Connor and Jones in the Joplin Hotel barbershop and stoically announced that he was obligated to serve a copy of the petition for $20,000 in damages to them as partners of the defendant hotel company.

"What's that—a $20,000 damage suit!" gasped Jones.

"What is it?" demanded Connor, as the deputy walked away, leaving Jones reading over the petition, which the attorney had made very lengthy.

"Thunderation!" boomed Jones.

"Consternation!" echoed Connor, with a look of dismay as he walked away. Apparently, Connor then left on a month-long vacation without a word, allowing Jones to believe the lawsuit was genuine. It also shows the latitude Joplin's early wealthy men were given.

By 1906, the Joplin Hotel was no longer the largest or most stylish hotel in town. Connor made the decision to replace it with a newer hotel that year. The new Joplin Hotel was much larger, with nine stories and a total of four hundred rooms. The new Joplin Hotel was to be the most opulent and impressive hotel in the city. Unfortunately, Thomas Connor didn't live to see the opening of the hotel that would ultimately come to bear his name. In 1907, shortly before the completion of the new hotel, Connor passed away at a sanatorium in Texas from an undisclosed illness. His family supervised the completion of the hotel, which cost a total of $750,000, and the name was changed to the Connor Hotel in his memory. Two workmen were killed during the construction of the Connor Hotel. One man was on the boom of a crane on the southwest corner of the building when the crane collapsed, sending the boom into the Club Theater on the southwest corner of Wall and Fourth Streets. Another man fell to his death in the elevator shaft as he walked across a ladder laid across the opening.

One of the two elevators in the Connor Hotel where a man was killed during the construction of the hotel when he slipped and fell off a ladder laid across the open shaft. *Courtesy of the Joplin Public Library.*

The lobby featured a white marble stairway beneath an open marble mezzanine ring that was enhanced by a

Vintage postcard of the Connor Hotel with a bi-wing plane flying overhead. *Courtesy of the author.*

crystal chandelier. Originally, the hotel featured a Louis XVI–style dining room, an Italian garden café, a newsstand, a billiard room, a smokers' store and a barbershop that also featured white marble decoration and French beveled mirrors. An auditorium seated two hundred persons and had a dance floor with an elevated bandstand. The glassed-in roof garden hosted numerous evening parties. In 1914, the hotel rates at the Connor were one dollar and up.

As with many public sites and businesses, reports from many claiming the hotel was haunted were downplayed by management over the years. But as with many sites, tidbits do leak out occasionally. Ward Provance retired in 1963 after working at the Connor Hotel for fifty-two years, outlasting thirty-two hotel mangers. He saw numerous celebrities walk in and out of the Connor's lobby as he rose through the ranks. He started as an elevator operator at the age of seventeen and then became a bellhop. Eventually, he became the superintendent of service. He kept mementos of some of those celebrity moments, such as the personal autograph of famed boxer Jack Dempsey, written on Connor Hotel letterhead. There were, however, darker moments he was privy to as well:

> *There were at least ten suicides in the hotel during my stay there, and never will I forget the day the nice-looking lady rented a room on the eighth floor. She ordered a chocolate malt, drank it, opened the window and jumped out. Another time I had to crawl through the transom of the locked door to see why this man had not left his room for three days. He'd taken poison.*

The Connor Hotel slowly declined during the 1960s and closed in 1969. Some businesses struggled to remain open in the building; the last, a restaurant, closed in 1977. The owners at that time had struggled for several years to keep the building open and functioning. Soon after, the Connor Hotel, once opulent and the symbol of Joplin's prosperity, became a victim of urban renewal and public tragedy. While the suicides that Ward Provance recalled were private tragedies that were kept behind closed doors, this last one was very public.

The work crew prepared the building for demolition by weakening structural columns so that the building would fall in on itself and minimize damage to surrounding buildings. The demolition was hyped as progress, and plans for the new Joplin Public Library were meant to reassure the public of the soundness of the plan. There was a segment of the population who disagreed with this plan, favoring a restoration of the Connor instead.

A view of a suite in the Connor Hotel in its heyday. Perhaps this is where a woman ordered and drank her chocolate shake before jumping from one of the hotel's windows. *Courtesy of the Joplin Public Library.*

The Connor Hotel as it appeared shortly before its collapse in one of the last images taken of the exterior. *Courtesy of the author.*

Perhaps ten years later the preservation voices would have won out and such tragedy would have been avoided. It seemed the building refused to go quietly. On Saturday, November 11, 1978, while workers went about their duties preparing to bring the building down, fate interceded. The preparations were almost complete and all that was left to do was to notch some of the structural steel beams and remove equipment from the building. The plan was for a festive occasion. The two companies handling the demolition had sent out private invitations to a dance in honor of the Connor Hotel for that night, as well as a Sunday morning breakfast from 6:30 a.m. to 7:30 a.m. The hotel's demolition would follow.

Shortly before 9:00 a.m., a handful of men were still finishing preparation for the implosion, including Al Summers, who was notching steel beams in the basement, and Thomas Edward Oakes and Frederick C. Coe III, both of whom were working on the first floor. All three men were on the south side of the building. A loud rumble came from above the men, and they were immediately imprisoned in tons of rubble of concrete, steel and plaster. Thousands of people responded to the disaster, and a portable seismic system was brought in to detect vibrations in the rubble should there be survivors tapping on rubble. Al Summers lived to tell the tale of his entombment.

Photograph taken in preparation for demolition of the Connor Hotel in 1978. The lobby looked much as it did when the hotel opened in 1907. *Courtesy of the author.*

Photograph taken in preparation for demolition of the Connor Hotel in 1978. The circular railing looked out over the lobby. *Courtesy of the author.*

He spent three and a half days encased in a space that was approximately two and a half feet high and had lost track of time. Upon his rescue, he estimated he had been buried about a day and a half. Oakes and Coe were not as fortunate. Their bodies were recovered two days later.

Rubble was removed to make construction of the new library possible. The Connor had three basement levels, and some of the rubble was left in the crater so the library could be built on top. The library, however, does not sit on the same footprint of the Connor Hotel, so the comparison of the two buildings must be taken into account when trying to determine the location of particular rooms or parts of the Connor Hotel.

Many people find it unusual for there to be ghosts or paranormal activity in a newer building where no deaths have occurred. It is not uncommon for paranormal activity connected to a location or building to remain after that building is torn down or after the site has been changed dramatically. So it is not surprising that employees and volunteers at the new library began having unusual experiences that, over time, appeared to be paranormal in nature.

HAUNTED JOPLIN

Paranormal Science Lab conducted an investigation of the library and was able to speak with library staff at length. It appears that multiple phenomena occur there, all of which may be related to different events in the past. The southeast portion of the building is reported to have poltergeist activity. In this area, employees and volunteers encounter books that fall off the shelves without explanation. Upon investigation, the shelving is heavy and secure. The books are shelved with a lip at the edge of the shelf, so it is unlikely that a shelved book would fall from a precarious position. The books are all very neatly aligned in uniform rows.

Given the frequency of this activity, it seems unlikely that random, misplaced books are just falling off shelves. Books are known to fall off of book trucks (rolling carts that hold books until they are shelved) as well. There are also phantom dropped books, where the sound of a book falling to the floor is heard, but when a librarian investigates, he or she finds nothing. When asked what their theory is as to what or who may be responsible for these dropped books, members of the staff smile and joke that it must be "one of the librarians." There are a couple of librarians who have worked at

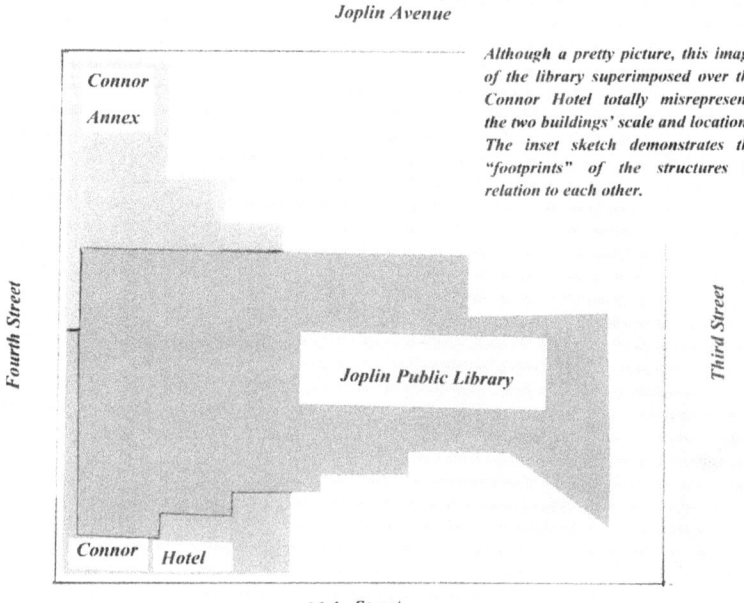

Although a pretty picture, this image of the library superimposed over the Connor Hotel totally misrepresents the two buildings' scale and locations. The inset sketch demonstrates the "footprints" of the structures in relation to each other.

This diagram shows how the Joplin Public Library overlaps the footprint of the Connor Hotel and provides a reference point for determining where locations within the library correspond to locations in the Connor Hotel. *Courtesy of Leslie Simpson.*

Paranormal Science Lab conducting an EVP session at the Joplin Public Library. *Courtesy of Paranormal Science Lab.*

the library for a long time and who were particularly attached to the library. They have long since passed away, and it is thought that perhaps one of these ladies is continuing her duties. During our investigation, PSL captured audio of what sounds like a book dropping to the floor when no one was in that part of the building. The noise did not appear to correlate to cycles of the heating system or any other possible causes.

In this same general area, there have been reports of a shadow of a person along the outer aisle on the southeast side of the building. Related to this shadow person is the fact that staff and volunteers who shelve books say they encounter something appearing to cross their field of vision while in that area but that it is not seen as a solid mass. Multiple times during our investigation, a flash of light was observed between rows of bookshelves by several people. PSL's attempt at re-creating the flash of light was unsuccessful, and it was determined that it could not appear in the positions observed if it were related to light coming in from a window due to the angles at which light shines through the window. Flashes of light or spheres of light are not uncommon paranormal events. Theories vary as to the nature of these lights, but it is generally believed that they are a form of energy and may be a manifestation of an entity in the environment. Whether there is consciousness or direct interaction with the environment is unknown. In considering known deaths in the Connor Hotel, the area where light flashes were observed would roughly correspond to the area where the three men were trapped during the premature collapse of the Connor Hotel. Also, it corresponds to the front wall of the Connor Hotel, which was lined with guest room windows, and may correspond to a location of a suicide, particularly one from someone jumping out of a window; however, this is speculation, as the exact locations of the suicides in the hotel are not known. That being said, it is also our experience that ghosts are not fixed to a particular building, much less a room. It is possible that any ghost connected to events at the Connor Hotel may be found anywhere in the vicinity. Residual activity tends to be more fixed in location.

Another common clue that paranormal activity may be present is battery drain in battery-operated devices. PSL uses new batteries for each investigation in cameras, EMF meters, flashlights, audio recorders and any other devices. Battery drain should not be an issue with this practice, but there are certain locations where battery drain is widespread. This occurred at the Joplin Library with multiple cameras, flashlights and audio recorders, with several battery drains occurring simultaneously. The probability of that happening randomly is extremely low. Additionally, the area where the battery drain occurred did not have an elevated EMF field, nor was there any other explanation for the interference of electronic devices. The rationale for the connection between battery drains and paranormal activity is that ghosts use electrical energy to manifest, interact and make noise or speak.

Battery drain is also sometimes accompanied by a sudden drop in temperature in a defined area, which is also rationalized as a ghost pulling energy from the atmosphere in order to interact. Battery drain and drops in temperature can happen without the other as well. At one point, an EVP session was being conducted in the area where dropped books occur, and two cameras suffered battery drain at the same time. Our attention was diverted to locating an electrical outlet to plug in a video camera, and an EVP of a woman's voice saying "Listen" was caught on audio. At another spot in the building, the question was asked, "Is there someone else with you?" to which a male voice replied, "Who?" Shortly afterward, another investigator asked, "Did you build the Connor?" A male voice replied softly, "Yeah." The next question was, "Did you work in the Connor?" and a loud thud was caught on the audio, to which none of the investigators reacted at

Paranormal Science Lab member Bill Martin videotapes an EVP session while other members monitor EMF readings. *Courtesy of Paranormal Science Lab.*

the time of the recording. It was then followed by an EVP of a man's voice saying "No." During the same EVP session, a female investigator asked, "Is Mr. Connor with us here tonight?" An EVP close to the microphone on one video camera caught an EVP response, which sounded like a man who was drunk, slightly slurring his speech. The voice said, "Ahh, he and I have been known to…" The last few words were unintelligible.

During another EVP session, a female investigator asked the following question: "Is John Hively here?" Hively was one of the two men killed during the construction of the Connor Hotel. There was no response. She asked the next question, "Do you know a John Hively?" Approximately three seconds later, an EVP was captured of a man's voice replying "No." The voice was not heard at the time it was recorded.

At one point when everyone was in another part of the building, an audio recorder, which was sitting in the vicinity of where the lobby and elevators had been located in the Connor, caught the distinct sounds of a man whistling a happy tune. There was no man-made or natural explanation for this; everyone with the investigation team was accounted for in another part of the building, and the building was locked so no one could have come in without our knowledge. Later in the evening, a shadow person was observed in this same general area, walking from east to west with a brisk gait, as if with a purpose. As is characteristic of shadow persons, it appeared three dimensional and was not cast on a wall or the floor like a natural shadow. It did not appear to notice any of the living people and continued walking west and disappeared when it reached a wall crossing its path.

Several experiences at the Joplin Public Library indicate that paranormal activity may be present. There are certainly compelling stories from the site's past that make a haunting here possible. The activity observed is a good example that we cannot assume we are alone as we go through the motions of our ordinary day. We may well be sharing that space with ghosts from another time or even from another building.

CHAPTER ELEVEN
PARANORMAL INVESTIGATION METHODS

Paranormal Science Lab approaches paranormal investigations from an objective point of view. It is not assumed that unexplained events are paranormal in nature. Alternative causes are explored, and anomalies are considered to be paranormal in nature only if no other reasonable explanation can be found. All investigations are documented by video, photographs, audio and other methods. Various types of data are collected during investigations, including atmospheric conditions, temperature, air pressure, static and fluctuating electromagnetic field readings. Data is recorded and preserved in electronic files.

Experiments are conducted during EVP sessions where PSL members attempt conversations or ask questions. High-end audio recorders, which are often used by musicians, are used to capture EVPs in the form of disembodied voices, as well as other audio anomalies that are not audible at the time of investigation. Tools employed include various models of ordinary flashlights. They are adjusted so that the battery connection is almost complete but also where the light is not on. The flashlights are placed on the floor, a table or other furniture. The floor is slapped with force to ensure that vibration from investigators' casual movement is not sufficient to cause the flashlight to come on. As questions are asked, any entities that may be present are requested to turn one or more lights on for an affirmative response and to leave them unlit for a negative response. Questions are asked in multiple ways, so that for internal consistency, multiple responses are required, both affirmative and negative. PSL does not consider responses as an interactive exchange without consistent responses over an extended period of time (usually a minimum of a half hour) and with consistent responses on multiple flashlights of multiple models. An example of such sessions is on the PSL website at the investigations page for the Kendrick House. Consistent responses involving as many as five flashlights at a time have been documented over as many as seven consecutive hours.

PSL also conducts experiments on kinetic energy, exploring theories of entities using available energy generated in the environment that is not electrical in nature. Children's balls of varying sizes, weights and materials are used and set in motion during EVP sessions, while the floors are measured for uphill and downhill slopes to determine if movement occurs that cannot be explained by the physical features of the floor and room. Colored stickers are applied to the ball so that movement can be observed more easily on video.

PSL uses multiple types of cameras, including wide-spectrum cameras (commonly referred to as full-spectrum cameras), which are sensitive not only to visible light, as are standard cameras, but also to infrared light (utilized in night vision and security cameras) and ultraviolet light. This allows PSL to record portions of the light spectrum not visible to the human eye or standard cameras. Another type of camera used is a high-speed camera, which can record video at up to 1000 fps (frames per second). The accepted standard for recording real-time video is 30 fps, meaning that video at 1000 fps contains 33.33 as many frames as video recorded at 30 fps. The typical television program is replayed at 24 fps, slightly slower than real time. The human eye can perceive up to approximately 240 fps. This means that any movement faster than 240 fps will not be seen by the naked eye. When replaying high-speed video, the display rate is 30 fps, meaning that it takes 33.33 seconds to replay every second recorded. Every ten seconds recorded will take 333.3 seconds (5 minutes and 33.3 seconds) to play back. The video will appear to the eye as being in slow motion, but in fact, it captures movement that cannot be caught on standard cameras. PSL has captured movement appearing in a general human form that was not visible to the naked eye of investigators present or the full-spectrum camera recording at 30 fps in the same area of the same room.

PSL has also utilized a FLIR (forward-looking infrared) camera, which captures thermal images, specifically contrasts in temperatures of objects in the image. While heat signatures can indicate the presence of a living creature, human, rodent or the family pet, unexplained heat signatures have to be explained. Unexplained images of a cold nature are of interest to paranormal investigators, as drops in temperature are often associated with paranormal experiences,

Although I grew up on a farm with paranormal activity connected to Civil War skirmishes, the most intense paranormal experience I have had came years later, at a moment when the paranormal was far from my mind. In the midst of touring a house in Webb City with a real estate agent, the paranormal intervened. While standing in the basement of a turn-of-the-century, two-story Arts and Crafts home, I felt a thumb being pressed against the left side of my throat and four fingers wrap around and press against the right side of my throat in an icy grip. Then the fingers slid through my throat and out of the back of my neck, leaving a cold sensation through my neck. I didn't say anything as I walked up the stairs. At this point, the real estate agent spoke up and said, "I should mention that the house was used as a mortuary in the 1920s." I didn't buy the house and have wondered numerous times since what else has happened inside those walls as no one has stayed in the house more than a year or two since that time. This experience does illustrate that we do not control when we will encounter the paranormal or where it may occur. But there are many places around Joplin where ghosts are waiting.

BIBLIOGRAPHY

PRINT

Belk, Colleen. *Jasper County Missouri Tombstones and Civil War Data*. Huntsville, AR: Century Enterprises, 1990.

Bendelari, Arthur E. Bendelari Jig. Patent 1,020,878, issued March 19, 1912.

Brophy, Patrick. *Found No Bushwhackers: The 1864 Diary of Sgt. James P. Mallery, Company A, Third Wisconsin*. Nevada, MO: Vernon County Historical Society, 1988.

Bunker, Edward. *Education of a Felon: A Memoir*. New York: St. Martin's, 2001.

Cottrell, Steve. *Haunted Ozarks Battlefields: Civil War Ghost Stories and Brief Battle Histories*. Gretna, LA: Pelican Publishing, 2010.

Gilbert, Joan. *Missouri Ghosts: Spirits, Haunts and Related Lore*. Columbia, MO: Pebble Publishing, 1997.

Gilmore, John. *L.A. Despair: A Landscape of Crimes and Bad Times*. Los Angeles: Amok Books, 2005.

Bibliography

Greer, Lillie Johnson. *Through the Years: A History of Peace Church Cemetery (104 years)* [and] *Sherwood Cemetery (100 years) in Galena Township, Jasper County, Missouri.* Joplin, MO: 1961.

Harper, Kimberly. *White Man's Heaven: The Lynching and Expulsion of Blacks in the Southern Ozarks, 1894–1909.* Fayetteville: University of Arkansas Press, 2010.

Hinds, Bob. *Ozark Pioneers: Their Trials and Triumphs.* 7th ed. Willow Springs, MO: Bob Hinds Books, 2002.

An Illustrated Historical Atlas Map of Jasper County, Missouri. Philadelphia, PA: Brink, McDonough and Company, 1876.

Joplin Globe. November 29, 1978. Post Memorial Art Museum collection. Joplin Public Library, Missouri.

Just, Evan. "Geologist: Engineering and Mining Journal, Marshall Plan, Cyprus Mines Corporation, and Stanford University, 1922–1980." Oral transcription of history lecture as part of the Western Mining in the Twentieth Century Oral History Series, Berkeley, CA, 1989.

Knerr, Douglas. *Eagle-Picher Industries: Strategies for Survival in the Industrial Marketplace, 1840–1980.* Columbus: Ohio State University Press, 1992.

Krajicek, David J. *True Crime: Missouri: The State's Most Notorious Criminal Cases.* Mechanicsville, PA: Stackpole Books, 2011.

Livingston, Joel T. *A History of Jasper County, Missouri, and Its People.* Vol 1. Chicago: Lewis Publishing, 1912.

Livingston, John C., Jr. *Such a Foe As Livingston: The Campaign of Confederate Major Thomas R. Livingston's First Missouri Cavalry Battalion of Southwest Missouri.* Wyandotte, OK: Gregath Publishing, 2004.

Loftin, Bob. *The Tri-State Spooklight.* Joplin, MO: privately published, 1955.

Monks, William. *A History of Southern Missouri and Northern Arkansas, Being an Account of the Early Settlements, the Civil War, the Ku-Klux and Times of Peace.* West Plains, MO: West Plains Journal, 1907.

Bibliography

Musick, John R. *Stories of Missouri*. New York: American Book Company, 1897.

O'Donnell, Billy, and Karen Glines. *Painting Missouri: The Counties Plein Air*. Columbia: University of Missouri Press, 2008.

Offutt, Jason. *Haunted Missouri: A Ghostly Guide to the Show-Me State's Most Spirited Spots*. Kirksville, MO: Truman State University Press, 2007.

Orlet, Christopher. "The Thrill Kill Cult." *American Spectator Magazine* (February 16, 2012).

Randolph, Paschal B. *Ravalette: The Rosicrucian's Story*. Pomeroy, WA: Health Research Books, 1996.

Randolph, Vance. *Ozark Ghost Stories: Gruesome and Humorous Tales of the Supernatural in the Backwoods of the South*. 1944. Reprint, Forrest City, AR: Marshall Vance, 1982.

———. *Ozark Magic and Folklore*. New York: Dover Publications, 1964.

Schrantz, Ward L. *Jasper County, Missouri, in the Civil War*. 1923. Reprint, Carthage: Carthage, Missouri Kiwanis Club, 2010.

Schroeder, Walter A. Introduction in *Missouri: The WPA Guide to the "Show Me" State*, by Howard W. Marshall. St. Louis: Missouri Historical Society Press, 1998. First published 1941 by Duell, Sloan and Pearce.

Shaner, Dolph. *The Story of Joplin*. New York: Stratford House, 1948.

Shoemaker, Floyd Calvin. *Missouri and Missourians: Land of Contrasts and People of Achievements*. Vol. 1. Chicago: Lewis Publishing, 1943.

Simpson, Leslie. *Postcard History Series: Joplin*. Charleston, SC: Arcadia Publishing, 2011.

Steele, Phillip W., and Steve Cottrell. *Civil War in the Ozarks*. 6th edition. Gretna, LA: Pelican Publishing, 2003.

Bibliography

Stephens, Mrs. Ann S. *Pictorial History of the War for the Union*. Cincinnati, OH: James R. Hawley Publisher, 1863.

Stephens v. Fire Ass'n of Philadelphia. 123 S.W., 63. Springfield Court of Appeals, Missouri. December 6, 1909.

Stevens, Walter Barlow. *Missouri, the Center State: 1821–1915*. 3 vols. Chicago: S.J. Clarke Publishing, 1915.

Tremeear, Janice. *Missouri's Haunted Route 66: Ghosts Along the Mother Road*. Charleston, SC: The History Press, 2010.

VanGilder, Marvin L. *Jasper County: The First Two Hundred Years*. Rich Hill, MO: Bell Books, 1995.

Wood, Larry. "Buried Alive." *Guideposts Magazine* (March 1980)

———. *The Civil War on the Lower Kansas-Missouri Border*. Second Edition. Joplin, MO: Hickory Press, 2003.

———. *Other Noted Guerrillas of the Civil War in Missouri*. Joplin, MO: Hickory Press, 2007.

Websites

"Bonnie and Clyde." Federal Bureau of Investigation. Accessed 2012. http://www.fbi.gov/about-us/history/famous-cases/bonnie-and-clyde.

"Bonnie and Clyde Garage Apartment National Register of Historic Places Form." National Park Service, National Register of Historic Places. Accessed April 1, 2009. http://www.nps.gov/history/nr/feature/weekly_features/BonnieClydeApartment.pdf.

"Community in Conflict: The Impact of the Civil War in the Ozarks." Springfield/Greene County Library. Last modified 2012. http://www.ozarkscivilwar.org/archives/1140.

BIBLIOGRAPHY

Cope, Louis W. "Jigs: The Forgotten Machine." *Engineering and Mining Journal* (August 2000). http://www.highbeam.com/publications/engineering-and-mining-journal.

"The Doors—Riders on the Storm—Lyrics Meaning." Music Banter. Accessed March 2012. http://www.musicbanter.com/lyrics/The-Doors-Riders-on-the-Storm.html#ixzz1qm5E2rFK.

Douglas, Julie. "Exploring a Haunted History." *Missouri Humanities Council News*. November 2012. http://www.mohumanities.org/news-updates/missouri-passages/november-2010-vol-7-no-9/exploring-a-haunted-history/.

Historic Joplin. Last modified 2012. http://www.historicjoplin.org/.

Joplin, Missouri Public Library. Last modified 2012. http://www.joplinpubliclibrary.org/.

"Kansas City Massacre—Pretty Boy Floyd." Federal Bureau of Investigations. Accessed March 2012. http://www.fbi.gov/about-us/history/famous-cases/kansas-city-massacre-pretty-boy-floyd.

"Kansas Legends: A Murderous Tale of Scandal & Treasure in Galena." Legends of America. Last modified 2012. http://www.legendsofamerica.com/ks-galenatreasure.html.

Missouri Digital Heritage database. Missouri State Archives. Last modified 2012. http://www.sos.mo.gov/mdh/.

"Odorant History." USA Pro Shoreline. Accessed May 21, 2012. http://www.usaproshoreline.com/pdf/odorant_historyoriginal-automotive_final.pdf.

Paranormal Science Lab. Last modified 2012. www.paranormalsciencelab.com.

Prosperity School Bed & Breakfast. Last modified 2012. http://www.prosperitybandb.com/.

BIBLIOGRAPHY

"Spooklight." Native American Research and Historical Preservation Society. Last modified March 2009. http://www.nativeamericanresearch.org/.

Spooklight Page. Last modified February 2009. http://thespooklightpage.com/.

Springfield-Greene County, Missouri online local history collection. Last modified 2012. http://thelibrary.springfield.missouri.org/lochist/.

"Theories About the Lights." Astronomy Café. Last modified 2001. http://www.astronomycafe.net/weird/lights/hornet15.htm.

Tri-State Spooklight Booklet. Joplin, MO: 1955. Scanned images of booklet, May 2002. http://inamidst.com/lights/spooklet.

USA Today "Fast Flying Bugs, Slow Cooling Earth." April 2005. http://www.usatoday.com/tech/columnist/aprilholladay/2005-02-11-wonderquest_x.htm.

About the Author

Courtesy of Paranormal Science Lab.

Lisa Livingston-Martin is a lifelong resident of southwest Missouri and currently lives in Webb City, Missouri. She graduated from Missouri State University with a BS in political science and earned a JD from Washington University in St. Louis. Lisa has practiced law in southwest Missouri for more than twenty years and is also a co-team leader of Paranormal Science Lab, which focuses on paranormal research at historic sites. She is the author of *Civil War Ghosts of Southwest Missouri*, also from The History Press.

Visit us at
www.historypress.net

This title is also available as an e-book

www.ingramcontent.com/pod-product-compliance
Lightning Source LLC
Chambersburg PA
CBHW042143160426
43201CB00022B/2389